Editorial Project Manager
Lorin E. Klistoff, M.A.

Editor-in-Chief
Sharon Coan, M.S. Ed.

Illustrator
Renée Christine Yates

Cover Artist
Barb Lorseyedi

Art Coordinator
Kevin Barnes

Imaging
James Edward Grace
Alfred Lau

Product Manager
Phil Garcia

Publisher
Mary D. Smith, M.S. Ed.

Author

Jodene Lynn Smith, M.A.

Teacher Created Resources, Inc.
12621 Western Avenue
Garden Grove, CA 92841
www.teachercreated.com

ISBN: 978-0-7439-3706-1

©2003 Teacher Created Resources, Inc.
Reprinted, 2019
Made in U.S.A.

Table of Contents

Introduction

Cut & Paste Science was designed to help the classroom teacher reinforce science content and vocabulary. After participating in activities related to each topic, students will have an opportunity to interact with the concepts and vocabulary by completing the corresponding activity pages. Hands-on activities coupled with additional practice using the activity pages will help students develop a better, deeper understanding of the science content.

Provided as part of the introduction are suggestions on how to use this book. Ideas on when and how to present the activity pages, as well as activities for introducing and reinforcing vocabulary are included. Following the introductory pages, the book is divided into four main sections: Physical Science, Earth Science, Life Science, and Health. Within each section, topics related to each area of science are addressed. The topics were selected based on standards commonly taught in the primary grades.

When teaching science content, a hands-on approach gives students a good foundation and personal experience with the scientific concepts. For each topic, a list of suggested activities is provided. These suggestions are ways to make the content more meaningful to students by providing activities, experiments, and projects in which they can participate in order to gain first-hand knowledge and experience with the concepts. Also included on these pages is a list of suggested books. There are many wonderful titles, both fiction and nonfiction, available that can be used in the classroom to introduce, reinforce, or review science content. The books listed are appropriate either for primary students to read themselves or for a teacher to use as a read-aloud. The authors of the books have presented the concepts in a comprehensible manner for primary students.

Cut-and-paste activity pages follow the introduction to each topic. Provided are three activity pages that require students to interact with the vocabulary or content in order to complete the page. The first two pages provide students experience in identifying, comparing, or classifying vocabulary or concept pictures. The third and final page within each topic has students using relevant vocabulary in order to complete sentences related to the content.

All students, especially English Language Learners, will benefit from the interactive way science content and vocabulary are reinforced throughout the contents of this book. Students must understand the vocabulary of science to fully understand the subject matter. The pages in this book were designed to provide a high level of interaction with topic appropriate vocabulary and content knowledge to promote success in science.

The book has been designed so that it is easy to use. Teachers will find the suggested activities useful for teaching science content. Students will find the cut-and-paste activity pages a fun way to interact with the science content.

Introduction *(cont.)*

The cut-and-paste pages in this book can be used a variety of ways throughout your unit of study on each science topic. When deciding how to use each cut-and-paste page, consider the activities you will be doing, the hands-on experiments, and how you will be assessing the unit. Listed below are some options, as well as times, for how to use the cut-and-paste pages.

Introducing the Unit

Reading a fiction story related to the topic or an informational book about the topic can be an excellent way to introduce science vocabulary. Once students have at least heard the science vocabulary in the context of a book, select an appropriate cut-and-paste page to use to reinforce the vocabulary words and science concepts. When the pages are used as an introduction to a unit, it is recommended that an overhead is made and the teacher work through the page along with the students. Students should not be held accountable for content knowledge or related vocabulary at an introductory phase of the unit.

Experiment Work Sheet

Many of the cut-and-paste activities contained in this book correspond with an activity commonly done in elementary classrooms. For example, in the section on "The Water Cycle," there is an activity in which students can make rain in the classroom using a teakettle and ice. There is a cut-and-paste activity ("Inside Rain") that has a diagram of the experiment on it. Students can complete the cut-and-paste activity as they complete the experiment. In this way, students have a way to remember the experiment they did, as well as the corresponding vocabulary. Check to see if the cut-and-paste activity pages correspond to any of the experiments you will be conducting in your classroom.

Teacher Lesson

In some cases, students will not participate in a hands-on experiment; rather, students will listen to a teacher lesson on the topic. At times, the appropriate equipment may not be available, time may be limited, or a teacher lesson is the best way to present the content information. Consider gearing your lesson around one of the cut-and-paste activities. As you present your lesson, students can actively participate by completing the cut-and-paste activity page. This is an excellent way to maintain student attention during a lesson, as well as illustrate concepts that you may be teaching.

Have students cut out the pieces at the bottom of the page before you begin presenting the lesson. Students should line up the cut-out pieces at the top of their desks so that they will have easy access to them during the lesson. You will also want to make sure each child has a glue bottle. Ensuring the students are prepared before the lesson will cut down on the amount of time taken away from the lesson later. As the you teach the science lesson, or as you read the book, stop at appropriate points to allow students to illustrate the concept by gluing the cut pieces in the correct places. Knowing they will have to complete the activity page will help maintain student attention during the lesson. By the end of the lesson, students will have a completed activity page that shows the content of your lesson.

Introduction *(cont.)*

Content Reinforcement

These activity pages can be used any time after a lesson, too. Used separately from a lesson or hands-on experiment, the activity pages serve as a way to reinforce content that has already been introduced. Students can continue to practice science concepts by completing the activity pages independently, in small groups, or as a whole class. You may choose to have students complete activity pages as part of a science center. For example, students can easily continue to experiment with magnets, even after the hands-on experiments or teacher lesson on magnets. Place the activity page on magnets, magnets, and the magnetic and non-magnetic objects listed on the activity page in a science center. Allow students to further experiment with the magnets in order to reinforce what has been taught about magnets.

Assessment

Of course, any of the cut-and-paste activity pages can be used for assessment purposes. Provide an activity page half way through your unit of study. Have students complete an activity page as a means for you to find out how students are understanding the science content and the corresponding vocabulary that has been presented thus far. When the activity pages are used as a monitoring device, your instruction can be altered in order to reteach concepts which students need to master but have not, or even to speed up instruction in areas in which students have a good understanding and are ready to move on.

The activity pages can also be used as an end-of-the-unit assessment to see if students have mastered the content area knowledge that has been established in the standards you are using. By having students complete an activity page as an end-of-the-unit assessment, you have a document establishing a student's understanding of the content on which he/she has been assessed. The document can be either sent home as a way of informing parents or it can be kept as part of a student portfolio. These documents can be especially helpful when it comes to assessing students at report card time.

Vocabulary Practice

The activity pages can serve as means to practice vocabulary as well. Scientific vocabulary is often difficult for students to learn. Often scientific words are unfamiliar or familiar words are used in an unfamiliar or very precise way. While students are completing the cut-and-paste activity pages, they are practicing scientific vocabulary in the context of scientific concepts. Consider using some of the vocabulary suggestions on the following two pages to help students learn and use scientific vocabulary more easily.

Introduction *(cont.)*

Vocabulary Ideas

Understanding vocabulary can be essential to a better, deeper understanding of a scientific concept. Use the following activities to help your students develop a better understanding of vocabulary words related to your unit of study.

Mini-Vocabulary Book

Create individual vocabulary books by following the directions below. Then, have students write one word on each page and illustrate the definition of the word. You may wish to have older students write the definition and/or a sentence using the word.

1. Fold an 8.5" x 11" (22 cm x 28 cm) sheet of white paper into eight sections.
2. Cut or tear along the center crease from the folded edge to the next fold line. (See diagram.)
3. Open the paper and push the end sections together.
4. Fold into a little book.

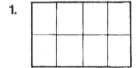

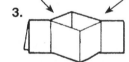

Quarter a Word

Choose a few words to "quarter" (shown below) together as a class or assign groups of students one or two words to "quarter." When the groups are done, they can report back to the rest of the class with their findings.

Students can either fold a piece of paper into four sections or draw a rectangle or square and divide that into four sections. In the first section, write the vocabulary word. In the second section, write a definition of the word. The definition can either be looked up in the dictionary or defined by the students. The third section contains a picture of the word. The picture can either be drawn or cut out of an old magazine. The final section includes a sentence that demonstrates how the word is used.

Vocabulary Word	Definition
magnet	A piece of iron or steel that attracts certain metals.
Picture	**Sentence**
	I picked up the paper clips with a magnet.

Introduction *(cont.)*

Vocabulary Ideas *(cont.)*

I Know!

Create templates students can use for the following format.

1. Write the vocabulary word.

2. Read the sentence where you found the word. Make a good guess as to what you think the word means. Write down your guess.

3. Look up the word in the dictionary. If your guess was right, check the box. If not, write what the word means on the line.

1. _____ My guess _____ I guessed right! ☐ Now I know it means _____ _____ _____ _____	2. _____ My guess _____ I guessed right! ☐ Now I know it means _____ _____ _____ _____

Dictionary Big Book

Divide students into groups according to the number of vocabulary words you wish to use. Assign each group a vocabulary word and provide each group with a piece of 12" x 18" (30 cm x 46 cm) white, construction paper. Each group must work to create a dictionary page that tells about the word they were assigned. Change the items required on the page according to the age group of the children with whom you are working. For younger children, you may only assign the word and a picture. For older children, you may require the word, a definition, the part of speech, and a picture. Display the dictionary pages on the wall through the duration of your unit of study or compile them into a big book.

Vocabulary Puzzles

People of all ages like to make and solve puzzles. Ask your students to make their own crossword puzzles or word search puzzles using vocabulary words.

Matter

Suggested Activities

Below are suggested activities that can be used throughout the unit of study.

- Begin your investigation of matter by having students bring an object from home. Each day introduce one or two ways to describe matter. Have students work in groups to observe their objects. Students should think of and record as many words as they can to describe their objects. Objects can be described by color, size, shape, and texture. Students can either create a table that shows the ways their objects can be described or they can write descriptive sentences. Display the students' pieces of matter along with their record of the descriptions.

- Help students learn about and remember the three forms of matter by teaching them the song "Matter."

Matter

(*Tune:* "Mary had a Little Lamb")

Matter comes in three forms,	Liquids can be poured,
In three forms, in three forms.	Can be poured, can be poured.
Matter comes in three forms.	Liquids can be poured.
I know them. How 'bout you?	Their shape is the container they're in.
Solids keep their shape,	Gases float and spread out,
Keep their shape, keep their shape.	Spread out, spread out.
Solids keep their shape.	Gases float and spread out.
That's just what they do.	Most are invisible.

- Provide a variety of solids for students to observe. Students will probably already have had some experiences sorting objects by size, color, and shape. Try to locate some objects that have a variety of textures. Students should sort the objects a variety of ways. First, students can sort the objects by size, then by color, then by shape, and finally by texture. After the objects have been sorted, have the students place all of the objects into one pile and think of a characteristic that names that one pile. Guide students to the understanding that all of the objects are matter and that they are all solids.

- Create a three-column chart on a piece of tagboard or butcher paper. Label each column after the three forms matter can take: solids, liquids, and gases. Throughout the unit on matter, list items that come in each form under the correct heading. Be sure to list the items that you use during experiments and demonstrations. Also, encourage students to use what they have learned about matter in order to classify other objects they think of. At the end of the unit, you may wish to provide 3" x 5" (8 cm x 13 cm) index cards with a variety of objects listed on the cards (or you can find pictures from a magazine). Have students work to categorize the items by solid, liquid, or gas and add them to the list, too.

Matter *(cont.)*

Suggested Activities *(cont.)*

- Provide containers in a variety of shapes and sizes. Gather several objects that are solids (paper clips, erasers, math cubes, etc.) and some liquids (milk, water, juice, etc.). Allow students to experiment pouring the solids and liquids from container to container. Help them determine that the solids do not change shape when they are poured, but the liquids take the shape of the container they are in.

- Have students experiment with the different textures of liquids. Provide a variety of liquids for students to touch such as liquid soap, oil, carbonated water or carbonated soda, water, and corn syrup. Describe the texture of each liquid. Try to sort the liquids into several categories. Provide a description for each category.

- Water comes in all three forms of matter. Demonstrate the forms water comes in by having students observe water as a solid, liquid, and gas. Provide a glass of water, ice cubes, and a demonstration of steam (water heated in a teapot). See if students can correctly categorize and describe each form of water. Create a chart on which students can record their observations. Be sure to have students describe the matter in terms of shape, color, size, and texture.

- Have students identify the ways water can change forms between solid, liquid, and gas. Provide students with an ice cube and challenge them to change it to a liquid as quickly as they can. Ask students how they can change liquid water to a solid. If you have access to a freezer, actually place a cup of water in the freezer. Later, observe the cup. If a hot plate is available to you, demonstrate how water can take the form of a gas by heating up water and allowing students to observe what happens. Students can record their observations.

- The water cycle has the potential to show water in all three forms of matter. Teach students about the water cycle. In what ways is water a liquid in the water cycle? In what ways is water a gas in the water cycle? In what ways is water a solid in the water cycle? How does water change from a solid to a liquid to a gas in the water cycle? What helps water change forms (the sun)? Lessons about the water cycle can be found on pages 53–57.

Suggested Books

Gardner, Robert. *Science Projects About Solids, Liquids, and Gases.* Enslow Publishers, Inc., 2000.

Mellet, Peter and Jane Rossiter. *Liquids in Action.* Franklin Watts, 1993.

Sarquis, Jerry. *Investigating Solids, Liquids, and Gases with Toys.* McGraw-Hill Trade, 1997.

Wilkin, Fred. *New True Book of Matter.* Children's Press, 1986.

Zoehfeld, Kathleen. *What is the World Made Of?: All About Solids, Liquids, and Gases.* HarperCollins, 1998.

States of Matter

Directions: Cut out the word cards at the bottom of the page. Glue the word cards in the correct places to label each object as a solid, liquid, or gas.

1.

2.

3.

4.

5.

6.

7.

8.

✂ -

solid	liquid	gas	solid
liquid	gas	solid	liquid

Forms of Water

Directions: Cut out the picture cards at the bottom of the page. Sort the forms of water into solids, liquids, and gases by gluing them in the correct places on the chart below.

Solid	Liquid	Gas

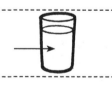

Matter

Directions: Cut out the word cards below. Glue the word cards in the correct places in order to complete the sentences.

1. ☐ is anything that takes up space.

2. Matter can be ☐ by color, shape, size, or texture.

3. Matter comes in three main ☐.

4. Liquids take the shape of the ☐ they are in.

5. ☐ have their own shape.

6. Gases float around and ☐ out.

✂ -

spread	forms	Matter

container	Solids	described

Magnets

Suggested Activities

Below are suggested activities that can be used throughout the unit of study.

- Provide pairs of children with magnets and time to explore. Have the students use the magnets to find magnetic surfaces in the classroom. Caution them not to touch magnets to computers, recorders, watches, televisions, etc., as magnets can cause severe damage and ruin these items. You may wish to provide a variety of types of magnets with which students can experiment, including bar magnets, horseshoe magnets, refrigerator magnets, and ring magnets. After a time of experimentation, create a chart listing the items in the classroom that had a magnetic surface, as well as items that did not.

- Help students learn more about magnets by teaching them the following poem about magnets.

Magnets Everywhere

Magnets are here, magnets are there,

We can see magnets most anywhere!

We find them in shower curtains, and even in cabinets,

Everywhere we look we see wonderful magnets!

They stick to soda cans, needles, and nails.

The strength of magnets just never fails.

Magnets are here, magnets are there,

We can see magnets most anywhere!

- Provide students with about four or five ring magnets. Have them hold a pencil vertically with the eraser end resting on a flat surface. One at a time, slide the ring magnets onto the pencil. If any magnet sticks tightly to another magnet, remove it, turn it over, and place it back onto the pencil. Discuss as a class or have students write about why the magnets did not stick together while on the pencil.

- Select a type of magnet to use for this experiment and attach a paper clip to it. Try to attach another paper clip to the first paper clip by touching the second paper clip to the first paper clip. Continue to add paper clips until the paper clips you are adding do not hold onto each other. How many total paper clips are hanging from the magnet? Can you hang more paper clips if you change the type of magnet you are using?

- Find out if magnets will work through water. Give each child a clear plastic cup half-filled with water. Have each child drop a paper clip in his or her cup. Ask the children to get the paper clip out of the water by holding a magnet outside the cup and sliding it upward with the paper clip hanging on. See if they can lift the paper clip out of the water with the magnet still dry.

Magnets *(cont.)*

Suggested Activities *(cont.)*

- Have students experiment making balls roll without touching them. Place 2–3 steel balls (ball bearings or BB gun pellets) in a box or dish. Pass a rod magnet directly under the box or dish. Observe what happens. What force made the balls move? Was the force strong enough to go through the box?

- Create a fishing game. Copy the outline of a fish pattern onto index paper according to the number of fish needed for your game. Slide a paper clip on to each fish. Then, attach a magnet to a wooden dowel with a piece of string in order to make a fishing pole. The fish can be programmed with any number of concepts such as the following: color words, contractions, addition facts, sight words, etc. Place the fish in a pond (a piece of yarn laid on the floor in a circle) and let the students go fishing.

- Have students make a magnet by holding a nail between a horseshoe magnet. Students should hold the top end of the nail between their fingers. Rub the pointed end of the nail across the magnet. Stroke the magnet in the same direction 30 to 40 times. Then try to pick up an item such as a paper clip or a thumbtack with the nail. Students can investigate what other objects can become a magnet. Have students use the same procedure while trying to make the following items a magnet: an eraser, a twig, a penny, a nickel, a rock, a piece of cardboard, scissors. Which items became magnets? Which items did not?

- Can you get iron fillings out of salt? Pour some iron filings into a bowl of salt. Mix up the salt and the iron filings with a craft stick. Pour the mixture onto a piece of tagboard. Suspend the tagboard between two stacks of books. Move a magnet back and forth directly under the tagboard. Can you attract the iron filings with the magnet and move them away from the salt?

- Investigate the origins of the compass; then make your own. Magnetize a needle in the same way as the nail was magnetized in the experiment on this page. Test to make sure the needle is magnetized by attracting iron filings. Push the needle through a piece of Styrofoam. Float the Styrofoam and needle in a pan of water. Watch how it moves. Once the needle has come to a rest, push in gently in one direction or the other. Observe what happens.

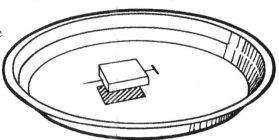

Suggested Books

Ardley, Neil. *Exploring Magnetism.* Franklin Watts Ltd., 1984.

Branley, Franklyn M. *What Makes a Magnet?* HarperTrophy, 1996.

Fowler, Allan. *Rookie Read-About Science: What Magnets Can Do.* Children's Press, 1995.

Krensky, Stephen. *All About Magnets.* Scholastic, 1994.

Olien, Becky. *Magnets.* Bridgestone Books, 2002.

Magnetic?

Directions: Cut out the picture cards below. Sort the picture cards between objects that are magnetic and those that are not magnetic. Glue the picture cards under the correct column.

Magnetic	Not Magnetic

✂ —

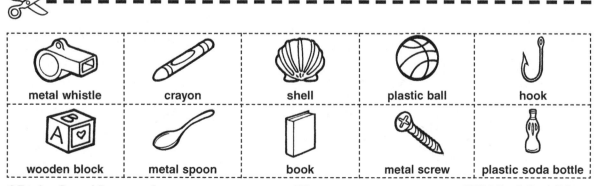

metal whistle	crayon	shell	plastic ball	hook
wooden block	metal spoon	book	metal screw	plastic soda bottle

What is a Magnet?

A **natural magnet** is a certain kind of rock. Sometimes this rock is called *magnetite* or a *lodestone*. Magnetite is found in or on the ground. Magnets can also be **manmade**. They are made of steel. Steel has iron in it. Man-made magnets are made in all kinds of shapes and sizes.

Directions: Cut out the picture cards at the bottom of the page. Sort the pictures between natural magnets and man-made magnets. Glue the picture cards in the correct column.

Natural Magnets	Man-made Magnets

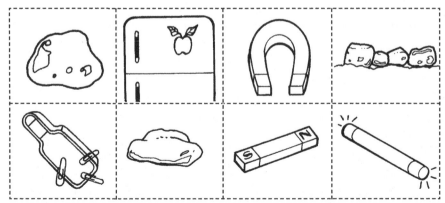

Magnet Vocabulary

Directions: Cut out the word cards at the bottom of the page. Glue the word cards in the correct places in order to complete the sentences.

1. Something that is attracted to a magnet

is _____.

2. To take away a magnet's force is to

_____ it.

3. To _____ means to push away.

4. To _____ means to pull close.

5. The strongest point on a magnet is the

_____.

6. A piece of iron or steel that attracts certain

metals is a _____.

✂ –

attract	demagnetize	magnet
magnetic	**repel**	**magnetic pole**

Simple Machines

Suggested Activities

Below are suggested activities that can be used throughout the unit of study.

- Display a variety of simple machines that we use around the house or the classroom which students can use to experiment. Be sure to discuss the safety of observing and handling these objects. Simple machines can include the following: scissors, nails, door stopper, zippers, screws, salad tongs, pliers, a bottle opener, tweezers, a staple remover, a pulley, and a jar opener. Challenge students to categorize the objects according to the type of simple machine they are.

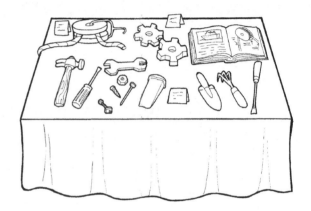

- Set up a variety of tasks students are can complete using a simple machine. For example, have students remove staples from a piece of paper using a staple remover. Then, have students complete the same task without the simple machine. Which way was easier? Which way took less effort? Were some of the tasks impossible without a simple machine? For tasks not possible without a simple machine, what are alternatives? (For example, if your jacket had a zipper and you could not use the zipper, how else could a jacket be kept shut?) Which way do you prefer? Tasks may include the following: opening nuts with a nut cracker, moving salad from one bowl to another with salad tongs, cutting a piece of paper with scissors, zipping up a jacket, etc.

- Demonstrate how useful an inclined plane can be in lessening the work load. Locate an area in your school in which you can create an inclined plane. For example, a sturdy board could be propped up against the stage in the auditorium. Be sure that the board you are using is sturdy enough to support the weight of a person standing on it. Caution students against trying this activity at home unless an adult is present. Then, provide a box of books for students to carry up onto the stage and back off the stage without the inclined plane. Then allow students to push the box up the inclined plane and back down. Which was easier? Why? Provide a dolly on which the students can place the box. Have them push the dolly up the inclined plane. Now what was easier? Why?

- Provide students with an experience using the simple machine, the screw. Locate some wood, screws, and screw drivers and allow students to experiment screwing the screw into the piece of wood. Have students observe which direction you have to turn the screwdriver to make the screw go into the piece of wood. Which direction do you have to turn the screwdriver to loosen the screw from the wood. How do screws help us?

Simple Machines (cont.)

Suggested Activities (cont.)

- A wheel and axle is most commonly associated with the cars. Demonstrate another simple machine using a wheel and axle by completing this activity. Tie a piece of string securely around a book, leaving about 2' (60 cm) between the book and the end. Tie a 15" (37.5 cm) dowel to the end of the string. Set the dowel between two desks so that the book is hanging freely between the desks. Rotate the dowel with your hands so that the string wraps around the dowel and begins to lift the book. Time how long it takes to lift the book. Next, tie a 5" (12.5 cm) dowel to the dowel to which the book is attached. Make the dowels perpendicular to each other. Lift the book again. Time how long it takes to lift the book. Which way was faster? Why? Try using a heavier book. What happened?

- Demonstrate how to set up dominoes in a line, so that if you knock one down, the rest will fall over, too. Allow students to build lines of dominoes and then knock them over. Help the students to understand that the dominoes act like simple machines. Domino sculptures are similar to gears in that they transfer the energy from one point to another. They do not in any way change the effort that you put in. You put work into the sculpture when you push down the first domino, and that work is transferred along the line. At the end, the same amount of work is present, pushing on the last domino. In this respect, it is like a simple machine.

- Bring a bicycle into the classroom. Have students identify as many simple machines as they can on the bicycle. Create a chart that shows the parts of the bicycle and the type of simple machine each part is. If you cannot bring a real bicycle to the classroom, provide a picture of a bicycle for students to look at or have them do the assignment as homework.

- Ask students to look around their homes and the classroom to locate other simple machines. Have them create a chart that lists each item, the simple machine(s) it uses, and how the item is used in everyday life. If students have a good understanding of the different types of simple machines, they will be amazed at just how much simple machines help make our lives easier.

Suggested Books

Barton, Byron. *Machines at Work.* Harpercollins Juvenile Books, 1997.

Fowler, Allan. *Rookie Read-About Science: Simple Machines.* Children's Press, 2001.

Macaulay, David. *The Way Things Work.* DK Publishing, 2000.

Nankivell-Aston, Sally and Dorothy Jackson. *Science Experiments with Simple Machines.* Orchard Books, 2000.

Wells, Robert. *How Do You Lift a Lion?* Albert Whitman & Co., 1996.

Types of Simple Machines

Directions: Cut out the word cards at the bottom of the page. Glue the word cards in the correct places to label the types of simple machines pictured.

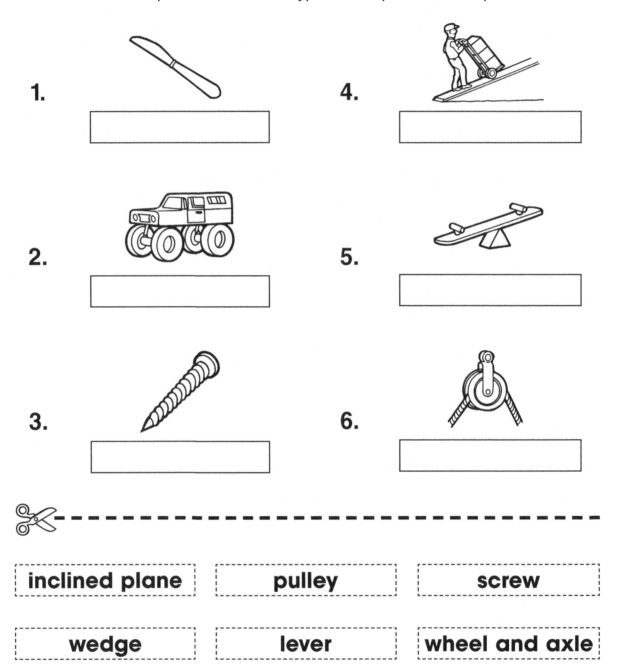

1.

2.

3.

4.

5.

6.

✂ -

inclined plane	pulley	screw
wedge	lever	wheel and axle

Around the House

Directions: Cut out the picture cards at the bottom of the page. Glue the picture cards in the correct column in order to categorize them as a *wedge* or a *lever*.

Wedge	Lever

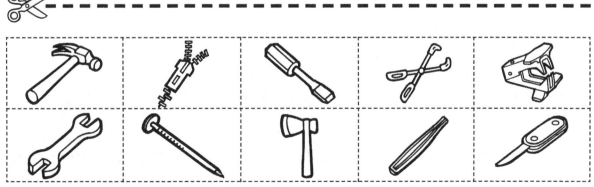

Simple Machines

Directions: Cut out the word cards at the bottom of the page. Glue them in the correct places in order to complete the sentences.

1. Simple machines help us do work with less _____.

2. There are six _____.

3. An _____ does not move in any way.

4. A _____ is two inclined planes put together.

5. The pivot point of a lever or the center of the pulley is the _____.

6. A pulley and wheel-and-axle are based on the _____.

✂ -

| fulcrum | inclined plane | wedge |
| lever | effort | simple machines |

Electricity

Suggested Activities

Below are suggested activities that can be used throughout the unit of study.

- Create a chart to list all of the items students can think of that require electricity. Add to the list as your study of electricity continues. Challenge the students to think of what alternatives can be used or were used in the past instead of electricity. List the alternatives next to each item on your chart.

- Conduct an experiment to see which brand of battery lasts longest. Obtain several brands of batteries and an object such as a flashlight (or toy) that requires batteries. If you have access to several of the same flashlights, you can test the batteries concurrently. If you only have access to one flashlight you will have to try one battery at a time and record your findings in order to compare later. Load the flashlight with a battery. Note which brand of battery is in the flashlight. Turn on the flashlight. Record the time the experiment begins. Keep the flashlight on until the battery dies. Record the time the battery died. Figure out how much time has past. Continue the experiment with another brand of battery by repeating the process. When you have tested all of the batteries, compare the amount of time each battery lasted. With older students, you may want to have them compare the amount of time each battery lasted with the cost of the battery. Is one battery more economical to purchase compared to how long it lasts?

- Have students experiment with static electricity by trying this experiment. Blow up and tie two balloons. Tie a piece of string approximately 1' (30 cm) long to the end of each balloon. Hold the ends of the string together in one hand. Rub both balloons with a wool cloth. Put the balloons together. Observe what happens. Separate the balloon and spray one of the balloons lightly with water and then put them together again. Observe. Next, spray both of the balloons lightly with water. Put them together again and observe.

- Observe the effects of static electricity on water. Rub a piece of wool cloth against a rubber comb. Turn on water at the sink so there is a gentle flow. Hold the comb near the water. Observe what is happening. Repeat rubbing a wool cloth against the rubber comb. This time, place the comb near some ripped-up pieces of paper. Observe what happens.

Electricity *(cont.)*

Suggested Activities *(cont.)*

- Test the following materials to see which will allow electricity to flow through them: a battery, a flashlight bulb and holder, three leads (with alligator clips or insulated wire with stripped ends), and a variety of different materials (paper clips, pencil, wood ruler, pin, spoon, eraser, etc.). Hook the alligator clips or wire leads to each end of the battery, one lead per end. Hook one wire that comes from the battery to one pole of the light bulb holder. Join the third wire to the other pole of the bulb holder. Touch the two unattached ends together. The bulb should light up. Disconnect these two ends. They will be used for testing the materials. Test different materials by connecting them to the two loose terminals. Students can draw a picture of their circuits. Try using a 9 volt battery and having students repeat the experience. Be prepared to replace the bulb.

- Have students observe what happens when a circuit is complete. Gather the following materials: two "D" cell batteries, flashlight bulb and holder, and two pieces of insulated wire 12" (30 cm) long with the ends exposed. Attach an exposed end from each wire to the two ends on the bulb holder. Taking the other ends of the wires, touch the bottom and top of the battery. Place the second battery into your circuit. Make sure the positive end of the second battery is touching the negative end of the first battery. Now place both positive ends of the batteries together and complete your circuit. Observe and then try to place both negative ends of the batteries and complete your circuit. Observe again. Have students devise as many ways as possible to complete the circuit with the materials they have.

- Allow students to control the electron flow in a circuit. Gather the following materials: several pieces of graphite from a mechanical pencil, three pieces of insulated wire 12" (30 cm) long with ends exposed, a flashlight bulb and holder, a battery, alligator clips, and clear tape. Using an alligator clip or a piece of tape, attach one wire to one side of the graphite. Attach the other end of the wire to one terminal on the bulb holder or wrap it around the metal base of the flashlight bulb. Attach a second wire to the other terminal on the bulb holder or tape it to the solder drop at the bottom of the base of the flashlight bulb, separate from the first wire. Attach the other end of the wire to one terminal of the battery. Attach the third to the other battery terminal with the other end of the wire exposed or attached to the other alligator clip. Slide the free end of the third wire along the graphite and observe what happens. Have students experiment trying other materials in place of the graphite. What happens?

Suggested Books

Bartholomew, Alan. *Electric Gadgets and Gizmos: Battery-Powered Buildable Gadgets That Go!* Kids Can Press, 1998.

Cole, Joanna. *The Magic School Bus and the Electric Field Trip.* Scholastic Press, 1999.

Evans, Neville. *The Science of a Light Bulb.* Raintree/Steck Vaughn, 2000.

Guthridge, Sue. *Thomas A. Edison: Young Inventor.* Aladdin Paperbacks, 1986.

Math, Irwin. *More Wires and Watts: Understanding and Using Electricity.* Atheneum, 1988.

Parts of a Light Bulb

Directions: Cut out the word cards at the bottom of the page. Glue the word cards in the correct places to label the parts of a light bulb.

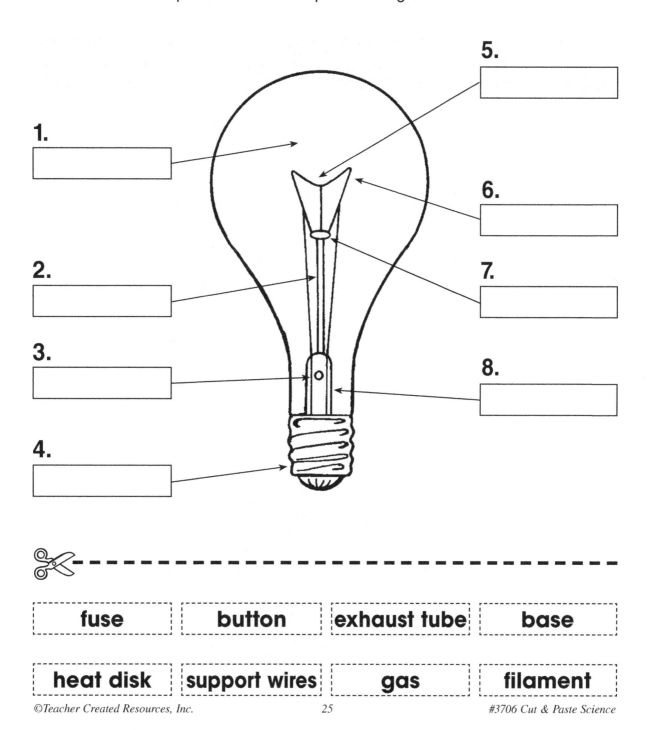

✂ -

fuse	button	exhaust tube	base

heat disk	support wires	gas	filament

Will It Light?

Directions: Cut out the picture cards at the bottom of the page. Glue the pictures in the correct column to show which connections will light the bulb and which will not.

Connections That Will Light the Bulb	Connections That Will Not Light the Bulb

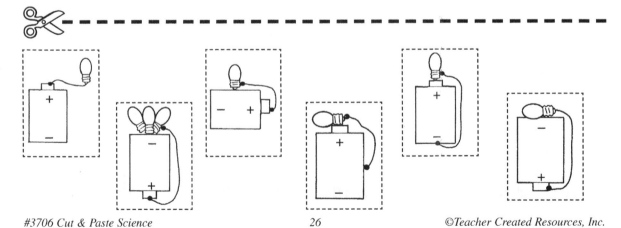

Electricity

Directions: Cut out the word cards at the bottom of the page. Glue the word cards in the correct places to complete the sentences.

1. The two types of electricity are [   ] and [   ].

2. The flow of an electrical current can be [   ] or [   ].

3. [   ] are materials that allow electricity to flow freely.

4. Materials that impede the flow of electricity are [   ].

5. [   ] electricity is formed when two objects are rubbed together.

6. A powerful form of electricity is [   ].

7. For electricity to flow, there must be a [   ] circuit.

8. Electricity can be generated [   ], such as a battery.

✂ -

| **static** | **Conductors** | **complete** | **direct** |

| **current** | **lightening** | **alternating** | **resistors** |

| **Static** | **chemically** |

Weather

Suggested Activities

Below are suggested activities that can be used throughout the unit of study.

- Go for weather walks. Observe and document a variety of types of weather. Have children draw pictures or write about the evidence they find which tells about the weather each time a walk is taken. For example, on a windy day students may observe the flag blowing, leaves blowing, and hair blowing. Allow students to try some of the activities below while on the weather walk.

- Allow students to experiment with the wind. Have them make a paper airplane or a pinwheel. (See diagrams for how to make a pinwheel.) Then take the wind toy outside to play with it. Record their observations on chart paper or have the students write about what they found out while playing with the wind.

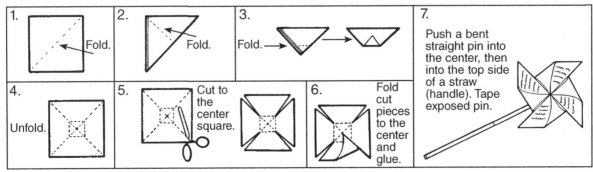

1. Fold.
2. Fold.
3. Fold. →
4. Unfold.
5. Cut to the center square.
6. Fold cut pieces to the center and glue.
7. Push a bent straight pin into the center, then into the top side of a straw (handle). Tape exposed pin.

- If you live in an area where it snows, take shovels and buckets outside and make snow castles. If you live in an area where it doesn't snow, bring in lots of pictures which show students what the weather is like in other areas. Be sure to include pictures of the types of clothing people wear when the weather is very cold. Try to find pictures of snow blowers and snowplows, too. Have students study the pictures and make observations about the snow. Record students' experiences or observations on a piece of chart paper.

- Have students experiment with the warmest and coolest places on the playground. Use a thermometer to measure the temperature in a variety of places including the following: the shade, the sun, on the grass, on the cement, under a covering such as a patio or roof overhang. Which is warmer? Which is cooler? Ask students where they would stand if they were feeling cold. Where would they stand if they were feeling hot?

- Take children outside on a sunny day and allow them to play with their shadows. After a time for experimenting, direct the students to find the smallest, largest, fattest, and thinnest shadows that they can make. Have them make their shadows go in front of them, behind them, and see if they can make their shadows disappear. You may also wish to show students how their shadows change throughout the day. Begin in the morning. Have children work in pairs. Using chalk, have one partner trace around where the other partner is standing. Then trace the shadow that is being cast. Alternate. Go back to the same place approximately every two hours. Have students stand in the same place. Trace the new position of the shadow with a different color chalk. Repeat.

‸‸‸‸‸‸‸‸‸‸‸‸‸‸‸‸‸‸‸‸‸‸‸

Weather *(cont.)*

Suggested Activities *(cont.)*

- On a rainy day, allow students to experiment with the rain. Using sticks, shovels, and dirt, have them build dams. Observe where the water goes once a dam has been built. What happens if there is a hole in the dam? Float a leaf along the water. Notice where the leaf goes. Of course, you will want to notify parents of your activity so they can dress their students appropriately. Teach students about tools used to measure the weather. Practice reading a thermometer in order to determine the temperature. Purchase or build a barometer and use it to figure out the pressure. Purchase or build a rain gauge and teach students how to read it. Have students practice making weather predictions for the next day.

- Record on a VCR tape the weather report from the local news or bring in the weather report from the newspaper. Observe and discuss all of the parts of the weather report: temperature, highs and lows, record temperature for the day, predictions for the coming days, barometer reading, and sunrise and sunset times. Have students document the weather for a given period of time (one week or one month). Young children can document whether each day was sunny, cloudy, windy, rainy, or snowy. Older children can record the temperature, barometric pressure, and rainfall as well. At the end of the period, have students look for patterns in the weather or temperature.

- Investigate the job responsibilities of a meteorologist. If possible, invite one to talk to your class. Record the weather report on the local news and show the tape to the children. Conduct a discussion after regarding the meteorologist's responsibilities. What tools does he or she use in order to report the weather and to make weather predictions? Are they the same tools you are able to make and use?

- Discuss the types of clothing worn in each kind of weather. How do we know how to dress? What do we need to consider when selecting clothes for the day? Guide students to the understanding that when the weather is hot, we dress cool; and when the weather is cold, we dress warm.

- Teach students about the water cycle. (See pages 53–57 for suggested activities and work sheets.)

Suggested Books

Branley, Franklyn M. *Flash, Crash, Rumble, and Roll.* Harpercollins Juvenile Books, 1999.

de Paola, Tomie. *The Cloud Book.* Holiday House, 1985.

Dewitt, Lynda. *What Will the Weather Be?* Scott Foresman, 1993.

Gibbons, Gail. *Weather Forecasting.* Aladdin Paperbacks, 1993.

Suzuki, David. *Looking at Weather.* John Wiley & Sons, 1991.

What Is the Weather?

Directions: Cut out the weather word cards at the bottom of the page. Glue the word cards in the correct places in order to label the type of weather shown in each picture.

1.

2.

3.

4.

| sunny | snowy | windy | rainy |

What Would You Do?

Directions: Cut out the word cards at the bottom of the page. Glue the word cards in the correct column in order to label activities you would do on a sunny day or on a rainy day.

Sunny Day	Rainy Day

✂ ─

Have a picnic	**Stomp in puddles**	**Wear rainboots**	**Wear shorts**
Use an umbrella	**Float leaves in the water**	**Go to the park**	**Climb a tree**

Weather Words

Directions: Cut the word cards out at the bottom of the page. Glue the word cards in the correct places in order to complete the weather sentences.

1. On a ☐ day, we like to go on a ☐.

2. When it ☐, I have to use my ☐.

3. I like to build a ☐ on a ☐ day.

4. I can fly a ☐ on a ☐ day.

✁ -

| rains | snowman | picnic | umbrella |
| windy | sunny | snowy | kite |

Seasons

Suggested Activities

Below are suggested activities that can be used throughout the unit of study.

- Help students remember the four seasons by teaching them the song "The Four Seasons." You may also want to explain that some people use the word *autumn* for fall.

The Four Seasons
(*Tune*: "Oh My Darling Clementine")

Winter, spring, summer, fall—

There are four seasons in all.

Winter, spring, summer, fall—

There are four seasons in all.

In the winter, trees are bare.

Snow is falling on the ground.

It is frosty; it is cold.

We have to dress in warm clothes.

Summer's hot and often sweaty—

Lots of time to go swimming.

School is out and it is playtime;

Sunny days are so much fun.

In the fall, leaves are changing;

They are falling on the ground.

It's a cooler type of weather—

Time for harvest and going to school.

Springtime's breezy and sometimes rainy.

It is green on ground and trees.

Baby animals are being born.

There is new growth all around.

- Adopt a tree to observe throughout the year. Several times during the year, at least once during each season, visit the tree to observe for changes. Have students bring a piece of paper and pencil and allow them to make sketches of the tree and make notes of their observations. During each visit, have students touch the bark, examine the leaves, and look for animals. Chart student observations which document signs of the season.

- Place a variety of clothing items suitable for each season in a bag or basket. Have students look through the clothing and sort the items by season. Since some clothing is appropriate for more than one season, students will have to determine the best season for each item. Once the items are sorted, students can choose a season and draw or write about an activity they could do during that season. For example, if a student chose winter, he or she could draw a picture of himself or herself making a snow angel while wearing gloves and a hat.

Seasons *(cont.)*

Suggested Activities *(cont.)*

- Create this art project to help students remember the four seasons. Fold a piece of 8 1/2" x 11" (22 cm x 28 cm) piece of paper in half and then in half again. Open the paper to reveal the paper with four sections. Label each of the sections with the name of one of the seasons. Dip a child's hand in brown tempera paint and create a hand print in each of the four sections of the paper. The hand prints will be the tree trunk and branches. Once the brown paint is dry, allow the child to go back and paint more detail to each of the trees in order to represent what the tree would look like during each season.

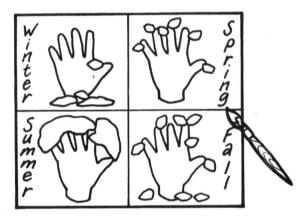

- Discuss how the weather is related to the seasons. In what types of outdoor activities do we tend to participate during each season? Brainstorm activities related to each season. Then have students select one activity and write about how the season and the weather relate to the activity. For example, a student may write about how he or she goes sledding in the winter time because it snows during the winter.

- Holidays are often associated with seasons. Have students brainstorm as many holidays as they can. Write down the students' suggestions on sentence strips or note cards. Assign each student a holiday to illustrate. Help the students categorize the holidays by season. Glue the students' illustrations to a chart which has been separated by season.

Suggested Books

Gibbons, Gail. *The Seasons of Arnold's Apple Tree.* Voyager Books, 1988.

Keats, Ezra Jack. *The Snowy Day.* Viking Childrens Books, 1996.

Foster, D.V. *Pocketful of Seasons.* William Morrow & Co. Library, 1977.

Rockwell, Anne. *My Spring Robin.* Aladdin Paperbacks, 1996.

Sendak, Maurice. *Chicken Soup with Rice: A Book of Months.* Scott Foresman, 1991.

A Tree in All Seasons

Directions: Cut out the word cards at the bottom of the page. Glue the word cards in the correct places in order to label the seasons.

1.

2.

3.

4.

| winter | summer | spring | fall |

Which Season?

Directions: Cut out the picture cards at the bottom of the page. Sort the pictures according to the season in which you would most likely do each activity. Glue the word cards in the correct boxes.

Winter	**Spring**
Summer	**Fall**

Dress for the Seasons

Directions: Cut out the word cards at the bottom of the page. Glue the word cards in the correct places in order to complete the sentences.

1. I wear mittens during [ ] to keep my hands warm.

2. In the [ ] I go swimming in my bathing suit.

3. I carry an umbrella in [ ] just in case it rains.

4. I wear a jacket in [ ] when the weather gets cool.

5. I have to wear a [ ] on my head to help keep me warm in winter.

6. [ ] help me keep cool on hot summer days.

7. A [ ] keeps me warm as days get cool in the fall.

8. A light [ ] helps keep me warm in the cool spring.

- -

winter	**hat**	**spring**	**jacket**
summer	**sweater**	**fall**	**Shorts**

Rocks and Layers of the Earth

Suggested Activities

Below are suggested activities that can be used throughout the unit of study.

- Bring a variety of types of rocks and objects made with or from rocks to display in the classroom. Some suggestions are: pencils, bricks, salt, chalkboard, chalk, jewelry, and concrete. Invite students to interact with the display by touching all of the objects. You may wish to begin a chart on which you list objects made from rock. Add to the list as your unit of study continues. See how many objects made from rocks you can find at your own school.

- Create a model of the layers of the earth in an empty gallon glass jar. Place a large, hard rock in the bottom. Then, layer different types and textures of soil (available at a nursery). Label the jar at the appropriate levels with the words *crust* (the rock) and *topsoil* (the layers). Explain that what we walk on most of the time is the topsoil of our earth. When we walk on a mountain or a big rock, we are actually walking on the earth's crust. Show the jar and discuss the above concept using the jar as a visual aid. Leave the jar on display for students to view.

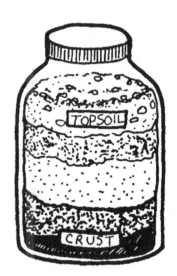

- Have students create their own model of the layers of the earth using a paper plate. Draw circles around the paper plate so that the edge of each circle is at approximately the following distance from the edge of the paper plate: 1/2" (1.3 cm) from the perimeter, 1 1/2" (3.84 cm) from the perimeter, 3" (8 cm) from the perimeter, and 4" (10 cm) from the perimeter. Have students label and color the various layers of the earth's surface.

- Rocks can be described and classified by how they look and feel. Use words such as shiny and dull, hard and soft, big and little, smooth and rough. Bring other objects that clearly illustrate the meaning of each word. For example, to illustrate the word *rough,* you may bring a piece of coarse sand paper for students to feel. Allow students to feel and look at a variety of rocks. As a class or in partner pairs, have students describe and classify the rocks. Display the classified rocks next to a card labeled with the description. Allow students to bring rocks they find to the classroom to add to the rock collection.

Rocks and Layers of the Earth *(cont.)*

Suggested Activities *(cont.)*

Illustrate the effect of weathering on rocks by conducting the next two demonstrations.

- Place fist-size rocks in a sturdy bag. Hit the rocks with a hammer five times. Allow the students to observe the rocks. Have they changed? How? What made them change? Record students' responses on a piece of chart paper. Place the rocks back in the bag and repeat hitting the bag with the hammer. Observe the rocks again. Record findings. Continue until the rocks become very find sand/soil. Discuss what happened.

- Put a handful of sand on top of a desk. Place a fan near the desk so that the breeze created by the fan blows across the sand. Turn the fan on low. Have students observe the effects wind has on rocks and soil. Record students' observations. Then, turn the fan to a higher speed. Again, have students observe and record their responses.

- Investigate animals that make their homes in the ground such as the following: moles, ants, and worms. What special features do these animals have which helps them live there? What do their homes look like? How have they adapted to fit their environment?

- Conduct an experiment with the three different kinds of soil: sandy, clay, and loam. Sandy soil contains large amounts of sand. Clay soil contains tiny clay particles. Loam soil has a large amount of humus (decaying plants). Allow students to touch each of the types of soil to become aquatinted with how each feels. Then, have students grow seeds in each of the types of soil to see which type of soil is best for plants. Observe the growing plants for several weeks. Record observations and findings on a piece of chart paper.

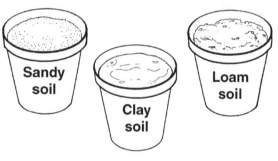

- Introduce older students to the ways rocks are classified: igneous, metamorphic, and sedimentary. Research to find what rocks fall into these categories, the characteristics of each group, and where these types of rocks can be found. Provide a variety of rocks for students to look at. Have students practice categorizing the rocks into these three categories by the characteristics of each group.

Suggested Books

Cole, Joanna. *The Magic School Bus Inside the Earth*. Scholastic, 1989.

Gans, Roma. *Let's Go Rock Collecting*. Harpercollins Juvenile Books, 1997.

Marzollo, Jean. *I am a Rock*. Cartwheel Books, 1988.

McNulty, Faith. *How to Dig a Hole to the Other Side of the World*. Scott Foresman, 1990.

Pondendorf, Illa. *Rocks and Minerals*. Children's Press, 1999.

Srogi, Leeann. *Start Collecting Rocks and Minerals*. Running Press, 1989.

Layers of the Earth

Directions: Cut out the word cards at the bottom of the page. Glue the word cards in the correct places in order to label the diagram of the earth.

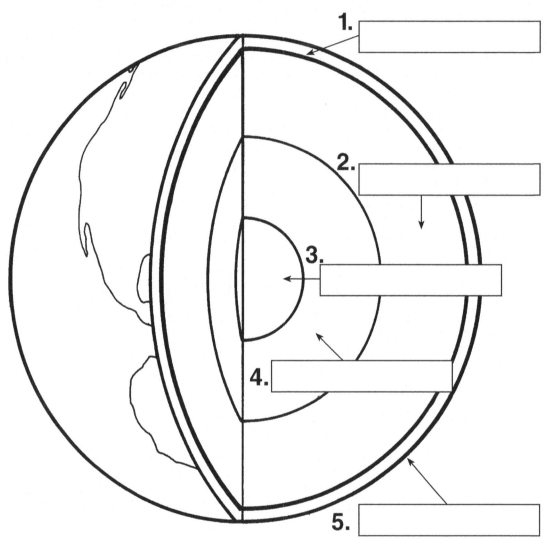

1.

2.

3.

4.

5.

✂ -

Topsoil   **Mantle**   **Inner Core**

Crust   **Outer Core**

This Is Rock?

Directions: Cut out the pictures at the bottom of the page. Glue the pictures in the boxes next to the word that describes how each is a rock.

1. diamond	**2.** chalk
3. lead	**4.** cement
5. salt	**6.** bricks

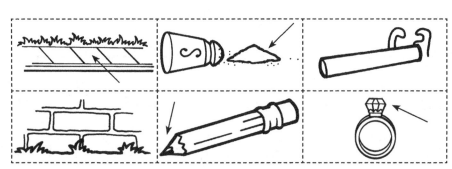

Rocks in the Earth

Directions: Cut out the word cards below. Glue the word cards in the correct places in order to complete the sentences.

1. [_____] is formed when rocks in the earth's crust melt.

2. Rocks can change through weathering and [_____].

3. [_____] is a very fine rock that has been broken down by the sea.

4. [_____] are rocks that preserve the remains of plants and animals.

5. The inner core, outer core, mantle, and crust make up the [_____] of the earth.

6. Rocks can be [_____] by how they look and feel.

7. A [_____] is a vent in the earth's crust through which molten rock and ashes are ejected.

8. Many objects we use are made from [_____].

✂ -

| **layers** | **Magma** | **Sand** | **rocks** |
| **Fossils** | **erosion** | **volcano** | **classified** |

Volcanoes

Suggested Activities

Below are suggested activities that can be used throughout the unit of study.

- Help students learn about volcanoes by teaching them the song "Volcanoes."

Volcanoes

(*Tune*: "Head and Shoulders, Knees and Toes")

Volcanoes form in the crust, earth's crust.
Volcanoes form in the crust, earth's crust.
Where there is a hole in the crust,
Hot rock in the earth comes out, comes out.

When it cools, the rock is lava, lava.
When it cools, the rock is lava, lava.
Once it cools, the rock is called lava.
When it cools, the rock is lava, lava.

From the magma chamber, comes magma.
From the magma chamber, comes magma.
When it erupts, molten rock comes out.
Very hot rock is spurt out, spurt out.

Mountains are built by molten rock, molten rock.
Mountains are built by molten rock, molten rock.
Hot rock shoots up out of a hole
And is built up near the hole, near the hole.

- Show pictures of the three different types of volcanoes. Using modeling clay, allow students to create their own volcanoes, choosing the shape they feel is most interesting to them. Group the finished volcanoes. Compare to see which volcano was made the greatest number of times, the least number of times, and if any were made an equal number of times.

Cinder Cone Volcano

(peaked)

Composite Volcano

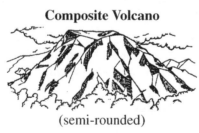

(semi-rounded)

Shield Volcano

(smooth and rounded)

- Explain the difference between an active and dormant volcano to students. An active volcano is one that is spurting out magma, causing lava and ash to flow down its sides. A dormant volcano is one that is not spurting out magma. It is said to be "sleeping." Using various resources, find out where active and dormant volcanoes are in the world. Use a globe to chart both active and dormant volcanoes. Use two colors of star stickers and attach them onto the globe at the locations. Have students create a key to the Volcano Globe. Place the globe and key in a location for all students to view.

Volcanoes *(cont.)*

Suggested Activities *(cont.)*

- Build a volcano model. Give each child a marble-sized ball of clay and a cone-shaped cup. Have the children put their names on the cups. Place the ball of clay inside the point of the cups. Mix plaster of Paris, about 8 lbs. For a class of 30, a little bit at a time, to the consistency of thick pancake batter. Put the mix into the cups and let set for 24 hours. Then give the children their volcanoes and several sheets of newspaper. Have them peel away the cup and remove the clay ball. They should have a volcano with a crater. Stand the volcano upright on the spread-out newspaper. Prepare the volcano for an eruption. Place about one

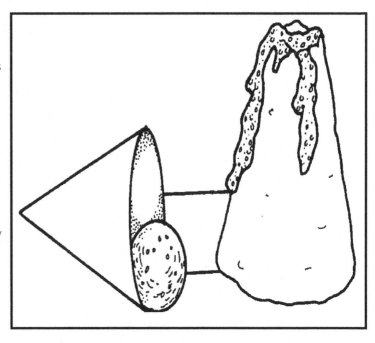

teaspoon of baking soda into the "crater" which has been lined with plastic wrap. Mix red and yellow food coloring with 1/2 teaspoon (2.5 ml) of white vinegar in a separate cup. Pour the vinegar slowly into the baking soda. Observe what happens!

- Show students a volcano erupting. Locate a video such as *Volcano*, a video of Patricia Lauber's 1987 Newbery Honor Book about Mount St. Helens or tape a news report about a volcano currently erupting in the world. Have students write about their viewing.

Suggested Books and Video

Ganeri, Anita. *Eruption—The Story of Volcanoes.* DK Publishers, 2001.

Merrians, Deborah. *I Can Read About Earthquakes and Volcanoes.* Troll Associates, 1996.

Nirgiotis, Nicholas. *Volcanoes: Mountains that Blow Their Tops.* Grosset & Dunlap, 1996.

Seymour, Simon. *Volcanoes.* Mulberry Books, 1995.

Sipiera, Paul. *Volcanoes.* Children's Press, 1998.

Volcano. (video) American School Publishers.

Volcano Diagram

Directions: Cut out the word cards below. Glue the word cards in the correct places in order to label the volcano diagram.

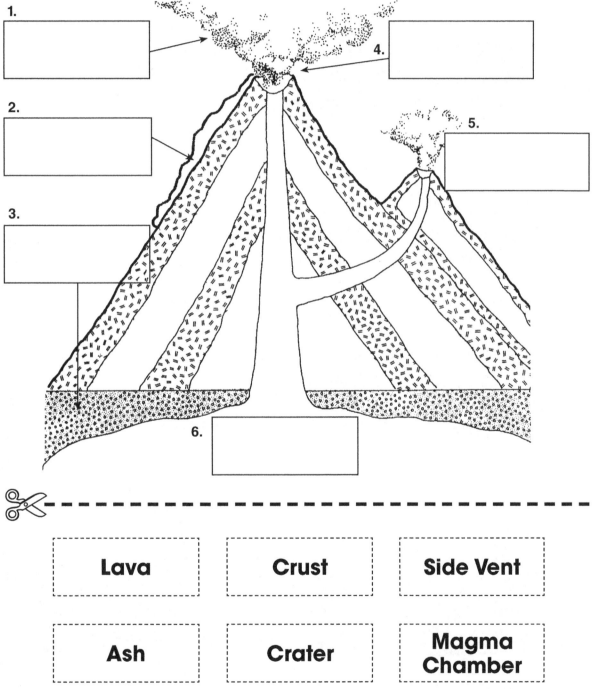

1.

2.

3.

4.

5.

6.

✂ —

Lava	Crust	Side Vent
Ash	Crater	Magma Chamber

Types of Volcanoes

Directions: Cut out the volcano pictures below. Glue each picture next to the description that best describes each type of volcano.

1. A volcano that is peaked is called a **cinder cone volcano**.

2. A **composite volcano's** shape is semi-round.

3. A volcano that is smooth and rounded is called a **shield volcano**.

Volcanoes

Directions: Cut out the word cards below. Glue the word cards in the correct places to complete the sentences.

1. There are three main types of _____: cinder cone, composite, and shield.

2. Hot magma is in the _____.

3. When magma cools, it is called _____.

4. Magma comes out of the earth's _____ wherever there is a hole.

5. _____ allow hot air and magma to escape from the volcano.

6. A _____ shows the opening of the volcano.

7. A _____ volcano is not spurting out magma.

8. An _____ volcano is spurting out magma.

✂ ---

| **active** | **magma chamber** | **crust** | **crater** |
| **volcanoes** | **Side vents** | **lava** | **dormant** |

Day and Night

Suggested Activities

Below are suggested activities that can be used throughout the unit of study.

- Go on a walk around the school. Have students observe the things they can see during the day. When you come back to the classroom, create a two-column chart labeled "Day" and "Night." Elicit ideas from the students of the things they saw during the day. As a homework assignment, have parents take their child outside at night (or once it is dark) to observe what they can see at night that is different from the day. When the children come back to school, complete the "Night" portion of the chart. Ask students what things they saw that were the same. What was different? How can they account for the difference?

- Teach a mini unit or simply read stories about animals that come out at night. Before you begin, have the students brainstorm as many animals they can think of that are nocturnal. As you teach the unit or as you read stories about night-time animals, add to the chart or, if necessary, cross animals off the chart. Learn about the special features nocturnal animals have that help them move around at night (especially eyes). Even though cats are not nocturnal animals, they have special eyes that help them see well at night. Have the children try to look at a cat's eyes at night. What do they notice? Have the children look at a person's eyes at night, too. Compare and contrast the similarities and differences between a cat's eyes during the day and at night. Compare and contrast a cat's eyes versus a person's eyes.

- Draw a line diagonally on a 9" x 12" (23 cm x 30 cm) piece of construction paper. Label one half "day" and the other half "night." Have students draw pictures using crayons to illustrate activities they do during the day and at night. Have students select one activity they do during the day and draw a picture of it on one half of the paper. Students should select an activity they do at night and draw it on the other half of the paper. Water down black tempera paint to about ¼ paint and ¾ water. Paint a wash over the "night" half of the paper using the watered-down tempera paint. The wash will make the night scene look like night. Once the paintings are dry, display them on a bulletin board labeled "Day and Night."

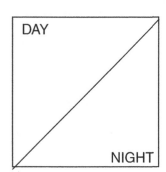

- By growing two plants, help students learn about one of the ways the sun helps us. Place one in an area where it will get sun and the other in an area where it will not get the sun (such as under a box). Observe the plants daily for about two weeks. Have students describe the plants at the end of the two weeks. What was the only difference between the two plants? Why didn't the plant without sunlight do well? How does the sun help us?

Day and Night *(cont.)*

Suggested Activities *(cont.)*

- Remind students that the sun gives us not only light, but heat too. Take students to a sunny place on the playground and have them sit there for a few minutes. Then, take students to a shady spot on the playground and have them sit there for a few minutes. When you get back to the classroom, record students' responses to the temperature in each of the locations. Ask students where they would sit if it were a hot day. What if it were a cool day?

- The moon is often associated with the night; however, sometimes it is visible during the daytime, too. Look at a calendar that charts the moon phases or look in the weather section of the local newspaper in order to determine a day the moon will be visible during school hours. Take students outside to observe and record their reactions. Then, for young children simply explain the moon is always there whether we can see it or not. There are certain times during the month when we can see it during the day, other times we can see it at night, and sometimes, we cannot see it at all. If you are teaching this unit to older children, you can conduct a more detailed explanation of the phases of the moon.

- Students are often very intrigued by both the sun and the moon. Students are fascinated that the sun is a star and equally as fascinated that man has landed on the moon. Locate some books on the sun and moon and read them to the students. Create a chart that shows how the moon and the earth are similar and different. What influence does the sun have on both the moon and the earth?

Suggested Books

Branley, Franklyn. *What Makes Day and Night?* HarperTrophy, 1986.

Emberley, Barbara. *The Moon Seems to Change.* HarperTrophy, 1987.

Fowler, Allan. *The Sun is Always Shining Somewhere.* Children's Press, 1992.

Gibbons, Gail. *Sun Up, Sun Down.* Voyager Books, 1987.

Rylant, Cynthia. *Night in the Country.* Aladdin Paperbacks, 1991.

Tafuri, Nancy. *What the Sun Sees, What the Moon Sees.* Greenwillow, 1997.

Day or Night?

Directions: Cut out the picture cards below. Glue the pictures in the correct column to label the most likely time of day each activity would occur.

☀ Day ☀	🌙 Night 🌙

✂ -

Day and Night Animals

Directions: Cut out the word cards below. Glue the word cards in the correct places to label when each animal is most likely awake.

1. dog

2. owl

3. butterfly

4. raccoon

5. opossum

6. horse

7. firefly

8. bird

✂ -

day	day	night	day
night	night	day	night

~~~~~~~~~~~~~~~~~~~~~~~~~~~~

Day and Night Facts

Directions: Cut out the word cards below. Glue the word cards in the correct places in order to complete the sentences.

1. During the [_____], we can see the sun.

2. At [_____] it is easier for us to see stars.

3. Nocturnal animals come out at [_____].

4. The [_____] is our light source during the day.

5. The sun also gives us [_____].

6. The [_____] gets its light from the sun.

7. The [_____] is sometimes visible during the day.

8. The sun is a [_____].

✂ ---

| sun | night | moon | night |
| moon | star | heat | day |

The Water Cycle

Suggested Activities

Below are suggested activities that can be used throughout the unit of study. Students will have a better understanding of how the water cycle works if they understand each of the parts of the water cycle. Activities that follow help students gain a better understanding of condensation and evaporation.

- Condensation occurs when a gas changes to a liquid. Students have probably experienced condensation when they order a soda at a restaurant. Help students understand this term better by providing a glass of water with a few drops of food coloring in it. Place 8–10 ice cubes in the glass of water. Wait a few minutes. Then observe the glass. Help students to notice the water drops that have accumulated on the outside of the glass. Explain that water vapor in the air changes to a liquid when it cools. Often students want to say that the water came out of the cup. Remind students that the water inside the cup was colored. The water that collected on the outside of the cup is not.

- Provide students with a bucket of water and paint brushes. Allow them to paint water on the sidewalk and side of the building. Observe the areas that were painted after a few minutes and then again after one hour. Help students understand that the water did not disappear; it turned into a gas and spread out. It evaporated. An alternative to this project is to wet a paper towel and hang it outside. Observe the paper towel after a few minutes and then again at one-hour intervals until the paper towel is dry.

- Create a demonstration of a cloud. Open a self-sealing plastic bag and scoop some air into it. Seal the bag. Put it in the freezer for about 5 minutes. When the bag is removed from the freezer, open it, blow into it, and seal it again. Observe what happens.

- Allow students to observe the water cycle first hand. This observation day will have to be scheduled on a day rain has been predicted. Arrange for children to wear clothing that they can wear out in the rain. Have students take a rain walk. Look for places the water is running off or collecting into puddles. Observe the same areas once the rain has stopped. Have students draw pictures or write about what they observed.

The Water Cycle *(cont.)*

Suggested Activities *(cont.)*

- Teach students the song "The Water Cycle" in order to help them remember the sequence of the water cycle and the vocabulary that goes with it.

The Water Cycle
(Tune: "The Wheels on the Bus")

The water cycle goes round and round,
Round and round, round and round.
The water cycle goes round and round,
Takes water all around.

First the water evaporates,
From the puddles, oceans, and lakes.
First the water evaporates,
Water evaporates.

Then the water condenses,
Condenses, condenses.
Then the water condenses,
Forms into clouds.

When the clouds get heavy, they let go rain,
Let go rain, let go rain.
When the clouds get heavy, they let go rain.
Rain fall comes down.

Once the rain comes down it runs off,
Runs off, runs off.
Once the rain comes down it runs off.
Makes puddles, oceans, and lakes.

Then the water cycle starts again,
Starts again, starts again.
Then the water cycle starts again,
It goes round and round.

- Create a rain demonstration in the classroom. Place a teakettle with water in it on a hot plate. Tell students that the water in the kettle is like a puddle of water from after a rain. The hot plate is like the sun. (Be sure students are a safe distance away from the hot plate.) Wait for the water to heat up. Point to the steam and explain that we cannot see water vapor, but it is just under the cloud. The air has already cooled the water vapor, and it is forming tiny droplets of water. The steam is like a little cloud. Place a metal pan such as a cookie sheet above the steam cloud. Put about 10–15 ice cubes in the pan. (Hold the pan with hot pads and avoid the steam.) Tell the students that the pan with ice is like very cold air that is found high in the sky. After a few minutes, drops of water will begin to form on the bottom of the pan. The droplets of water will begin to collect together. Wiggle the pan gently and the water droplets will fall, just like rain!

Suggested Books

Dorros, Arthur. *Follow the Water from Brook to Ocean.* HarperTrophy, 1993.

Hale, James Graham. *Down Comes the Rain.* HarperTrophy, 1997.

Schaefer, Lola. *This Is the Rain.* Greenwillow, 2001.

Spiers, Peter. *Rain.* Doubleday, 1997.

Wick, Walter. *A Drop of Water: A Book of Science and Wonder.* Scholastic Trade, 1997.

The Water Cycle

Directions: Cut out the word cards below. Glue the word cards in the correct places in order to label the water cycle.

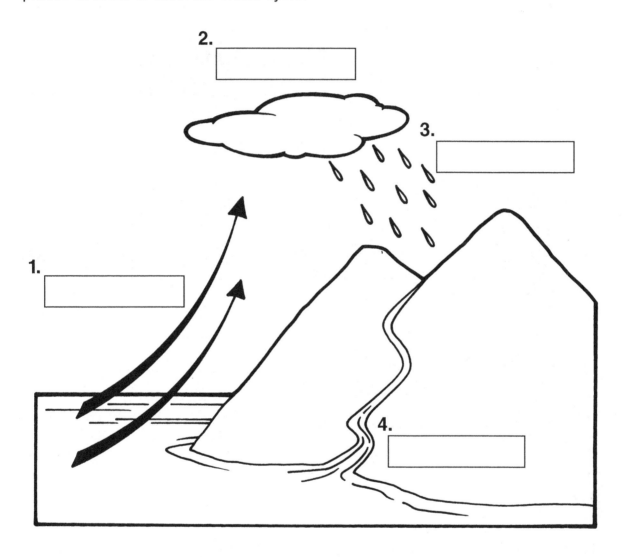

2.

3.

1.

4.

✂ -

| **evaporation** | **condensation** | **rain** | **run-off** |

Inside Rain

Directions: Cut out the pictures at the bottom of the page. Glue them in the correct places in order to label the diagram.

The Water Cycle

Directions: Cut out the word cards at the bottom of the page. Glue them in the correct places in order to complete the sentences.

1. Water on earth collects in puddles, lakes, and the

   ☐.

2. The ☐ warms the earth's water.

3. Water changes from a liquid to water vapor when it

   ☐.

4. When water vapor cools, it ☐.

5. Condensed water forms ☐ high in the sky.

6. When the clouds become too heavy, they drop the water as

   ☐.

7. Rain water ☐ to collect in puddles, lakes, and the
   ocean.

8. The changes of water are called the ☐.

✂ –

sun	condenses	rain	water cycle
runs off	evaporates	clouds	ocean

Plants

Suggested Activities

Below are suggested activities that can be used throughout the unit of study.

- Bring a variety of plants to the classroom for students to observe. Include a variety of plants such as ferns, flowering plants (pansies, marigolds, etc.), cactus, and even Venus fly traps. Chart students' responses as they observe how the plants are similar and different.

- Allow students to plant bean seeds (or other seeds of your choice) in a paper or plastic cup. Have each child fill a cup with dirt. Create a hole in the dirt by using the tip of a pencil. Drop the seed inside the hole and cover it with dirt. Water lightly and place in a sunny spot. Have students observe their bean plants daily. (Provide hand lenses for students to use when observing their bean plant.) Students can document the progress of their bean seed in a journal. Be sure to keep track of the date, when the plant was watered, where the plant was kept, the height of the stem, and the number of leaves.

- Create a special bean plant cup for observing the root system. Fold a paper towel so that it will fit around the inside perimeter of a clear plastic cup. Wet the paper towel so that it is damp. Place a seed in between the paper towel and the cup. Hold the paper towel in place while filling the cup with dirt. Water. Students will be able to observe what is happening to the seed "underground" as the seed expands and the root system develops. Have students observe this cup while they are waiting for their seeds to sprout or allow all of the children to plant their seeds in this manner.

- Demonstrate one of the functions of the stem by changing the color of a carnation (or a stalk of celery). Place about ten drops of food coloring in a vase with water. Cut a few inches off of the stem of a white carnation and place the carnation in the colored water. Allow the carnation to stay in the water for several hours. Have students observe the flower every few hours.

- We eat all of the parts of a plant: the seeds, the roots, the stems, and the flowers. Bring in a variety of fruits and vegetables. If you are able to locate a picture of the plant on which each grows, bring that, too. Investigate on which part of the plant each of the fruits and vegetables grows. Create a chart that shows vegetables that are seeds, roots, stems, and flowers.

Plants *(cont.)*

Suggested Activities *(cont.)*

- Use a pony pack of flowering plants in order to conduct this experiment with each of the plants. Separate the plants and plant each into a cup or small pot. Use dirt or potting soil to fill the cup so that the plant is appropriately planted. Demonstrate the needs of plants by doing the following to each plant:

No Air:	Place the potted plant in a jar with a lid on it.
No Water:	Do not give the plant any water during the experiment.
No Roots:	Cut the roots off the plant before planting it.
No Sun:	Place the potted plant under a box.
No Soil:	Shake as much of the dirt off of the roots as possible and set it in the cup. Do not add additional soil to fill the cup.
Air, Water, Roots, Sun:	Pot the plant normally and provide it with air, water, and sun.

Have students observe each of the plants daily. Chart the students' observations of each plant at the end of two weeks. Help students to determine the needs of plants.

- Observe a variety of different kinds of seeds. Bring a variety of fruits to school and slice each in half. Have students record the type of fruit, the size of the seeds and the number of the seeds. You may wish to grow some of the seeds from the fruits. For example, place three toothpicks (equidistant apart) in the sides of an avocado seed and place it in a cup filled with water so that the water covers the bottom third of the seed. Watch as the seed grows.

- Go on a leaf hunt. Provide each student or group of students with a brown paper bag and allow them to look around the school for a variety of leaves. After students have returned to the classroom, have them observe the leaves. Provide hand lenses for students to get a closer look at the vein patterns on the leaves. Have students sort and categorize the leaves. Then, allow students to do a leaf rubbing of one leaf from each of their categories.

Suggested Books

Carle, Eric. *The Tiny Seed.* Aladdin Paperbacks, 2001.

Gibbons, Gail. *From Seed to Plant.* Holiday House, 1993.

Heller, Ruth. *The Reason for a Flower.* Paper Star, 1999.

Rahn, Joan Elma. *Seven Ways to Collect Plants.* Atheneum, 1978.

Wexler, Jerome. *Flowers, Fruits, Seeds.* Houghton Mifflin, 1991.

Parts of a Plant

Directions: Cut out the word cards below. Glue them in the correct places so the parts of the plant are labeled.

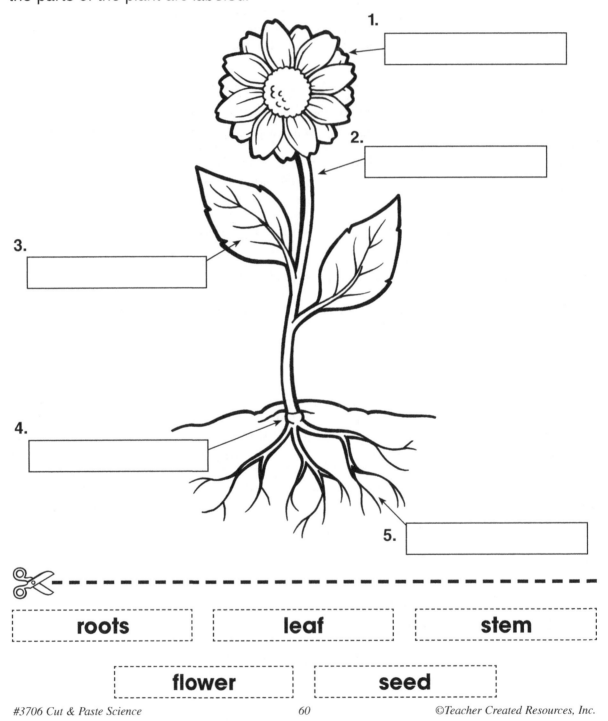

1.

2.

3.

4.

5.

✂ -

| roots | leaf | stem |

| flower | seed |

What Parts Do We Eat?

Directions: Cut out the picture and word cards at the bottom of the page. Glue them in the correct places to label the parts of the plant that we eat.

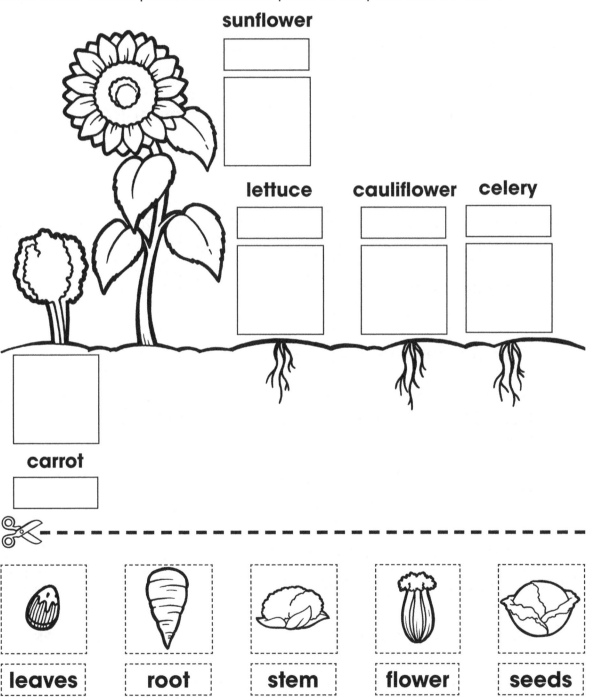

sunflower

lettuce   cauliflower   celery

carrot

✂ --

leaves   **root**   **stem**   **flower**   **seeds**

Plant Part Functions

Directions: Cut out the word cards at the bottom of the page. Glue them in the correct places in order to complete the sentences.

1. Plant a _____ to grow a plant.

2. Plants need water, soil, and sunlight in order to
_____.

3. The _____ take water from the soil for the plant.

4. The roots help hold the _____ in place.

5. The stem helps hold up the _____.

6. A _____ brings water up the plant.

7. _____ make food for the plant.

8. The _____ has new seeds.

✂ -

| roots | Leaves | grow | leaves |
| plant | stem | flower | seed |

Animals

There are two major divisions in the animal kingdom: vertebrates (animals with backbones) and invertebrates (animals without backbones). Students are probably most familiar with vertebrates; however, invertebrates make up more than 75% of the animals on Earth. Because this unit will be used with young children, only two classes of invertebrates are used on the activity sheets: mollusks and arthropods. The animals with which most students will be familiar within arthropods are insects.

Suggested Activities

- Create a chart on which students can categorize animals. The chart for very young children can simply be of animal body coverings. Create a column for feathers, hair/fur, and scales. For older children, use animal class for categorization (mollusks, mammals, birds, etc.). As you read stories or learn about animals, determine under which column the animals best fit and list them on the chart. Keep the list running throughout your unit of study and after!

- Research how animals are categorized. In small groups or as a class project, create a chart that demonstrates how animals are categorized. Be sure to include the following: Kingdom, Phylum, Class, Order, Family, Genus, and Species. Provide an example, too.

- All animals have the basic needs of air, water, food, and shelter. Fold a piece of paper in half and then in half again so that when it is opened up, there are four sections. In the center of the paper, each student can write the name or draw a picture of an animal. (Each child can have a different animal or the class can all have the same animal.) Each of the four sections should then be labeled with the words *air, water, food,* and *shelter* (one word in each section). Have each student list or draw a picture of how the chosen animal meets its needs.

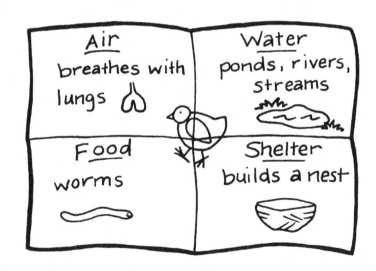

Animals *(cont.)*

Suggested Activities *(cont.)*

- List a variety of animals on 3" x 5" (8 cm x 13 cm) index cards, or, if possible, provide pictures of animals. Distribute them to the class. For younger children, select animals with which they are familiar. For older children, you may want to select animals for which the students will have to do some research. Have the students draw a picture of the type of shelter the animal requires. Be sure to have the students draw a picture of the animal in its shelter. Once all of the pictures have been completed, sort the animals by class. Look for patterns in the types of shelter required by each class of animal.

- Learn more about the invertebrate animals with which we are not as familiar. Have students research the following: sponges, coelenterates, echinoderms, worms, and even mollusks, and arthropods. Students should include characteristics of the animal grouping, as well as how each group's basic needs are met.

- Some animals, such as bats, rely on their hearing more than their eyes. Have students experience what it is like to rely on hearing. Clear an area in the classroom in which students can move about freely. Place five students around the room and number them from one to five. These five students need to determine a noise they will make such as singing, humming, or an animal noise such as barking. Pair the remaining students into groups of two. Blindfold one student (or simply have him or her close his or her eyes). The student numbered one must provide an auditory signal that he or she will sound while the blindfolded student makes his or her way toward number one. Once the blindfolded student has arrived at number 1, the number two student begins to make his or her noise. The blindfolded student makes his or her way toward number two. The blindfolded student makes his or her way from number to number following the auditory cue. The other student in the pair should follow closely to ensure the safety of the blindfolded student. Students can write about their experiences relying only on their hearing.

Suggested Books

Berger, Gilda. *Can Snakes Crawl Backward? Questions and Answers About Reptiles.* Scholastic Reference, 2002.

Boring, Mel. *Birds, Nests, and Eggs.* Creative Publishing International, 1998.

Nicholas, Christopher. *Fish!* Learning H, 2000.

Scarborough, Sheryl. *About Bugs.* Treasure Bay, 1998.

Sill, Cathryn. *About Mammals: A Guide for Children.* Peachtree Publishers, 1997.

Sill, Cathryn. *About Birds: A Guide for Children.* Peachtree Publishers, 1997.

Sill, Cathryn. *About Fish: A Guide for Children.* Peachtree Publishers. 2002.

Sill, Cathryn. *About Amphibians: A Guide for Children.* Peachtree Publishers, 2001.

Sill, Cathryn. *About Reptiles: A Guide for Children.* Peachtree Publishers, 1999.

Animal Sort

Directions: Cut out the animal cards on this page. Sort them according to the type of animal each is. Glue the cards in the correct places on page 66.

racoon	dragonfly	robin
shark	salamander	toads
hummingbird	elephant	snake
turtle	slug	butterfly
ladybug	eagle	snail
frog	lizard	trout
octopus	salmon	dog

Animal Sort *(cont.)*

Arthropods (Insects)	Mollusks
Birds	Amphibians
Mammals	Fish
A N I M A L S	Reptiles

Animal Characteristics

Directions: Cut out the animal type cards at the bottom of the page. Glue the cards in the correct places on the chart according to the characteristics of each type of animal.

Warm Blooded	Cold Blooded	Backbone
Lay Eggs	**Have Wings**	**No Backbone**

mammals	fish	birds	fish	birds	birds
birds	amphibians	reptiles	amphibians	mollusks	arthropods
reptiles	mammals	amphibians	reptiles	arthropods	fish

Animal Features

Directions: Cut out the word cards at the bottom of the page. Glue them in the correct place in order to complete the sentences.

1. Mammals have hair or fur. They feed on ☐ from their mothers' bodies.

2. Birds have ☐, wings, two feet, and a hard beak. Most birds can ☐.

3. Reptiles have scaly ☐. Most reptiles lay eggs, but some give birth to their young.

4. ☐ are cold blooded, live in water, and have scales, fins, and gills. Most of them lay eggs.

5. Amphibians are cold blooded, have a backbone, and can live in ☐ or on ☐. They lay eggs.

6. Mollusks have a soft body and no ☐. Some have a hard shell. They live on land or in water.

7. Arthropods have ☐ bodies. Arthropods have an ☐.

✂ -

land	exoskeleton	milk	water	segmented
skin	**spine**	**Fish**	**fly**	**feathers**

Insects

Suggested Activities

Below are suggested activities that can be used throughout the unit of study.

- Help students learn about insect features by teaching them the song "Insect Parts."

Insect Parts

(*Tune*: "Head and Shoulders, Knees and Toes")

Every insect has three parts, three parts

Every insect has three parts, three parts.

Head and thorax, abdomen

Every insect has three parts, three parts.

Two antennae are feelers, feelers

Two antennae are feelers, feelers.

Antennae are on the head

Two antennae are feelers, feelers.

Some insects do have wings, have wings

Some insects do have wings, have wings.

Ladybugs, and bees, and moths

Some insects do have wings, have wings.

- Provide pictures of a variety of insects such as the following: ants, fleas, mosquitoes, fireflies, moths, bees, flies, grasshoppers, butterflies, termites, crickets, ladybugs, and dragonflies for students to look at. Help students identify the head, thorax, abdomen, legs, and, if appropriate, wings on each insect. You may wish to also include some pictures of non-insects and have students distinguish the pictures between insects and non-insects based on what they know about insects.

- Purchase or find insects for students to observe or have students go on a nature walk in order to collect insects. House the insects in an aquarium; plastic animal cage; or if you are going to keep the insects temporarily (a day), in a jar with holes punched in the top. Allow students time to observe the behavior and characteristics of the insects. You may wish to provide paper for students to write or draw their observations.

- Create a Venn diagram in order to compare and contrast two insects. For example, students can complete a Venn diagram comparing and contrasting moths and butterflies. Write items that are the same in the overlapping section of the Venn diagram. Write items that are different in the outer sections of each circle.

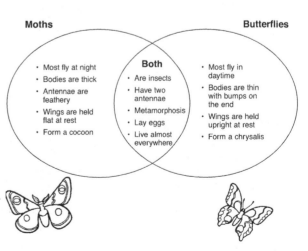

Moths

- Most fly at night
- Bodies are thick
- Antennae are feathery
- Wings are held flat at rest
- Form a cocoon

Both

- Are insects
- Have two antennae
- Metamorphosis
- Lay eggs
- Live almost everywhere

Butterflies

- Most fly in daytime
- Bodies are thin with bumps on the end
- Wings are held upright at rest
- Form a chrysalis

Insects *(cont.)*

Suggested Activities *(cont.)*

- Emphasize the three body sections of every insect: the head, thorax, and abdomen. Cut the tops off of egg cartons. Then, cut the egg cartons into three-cup sections. Allow each student to paint one of the sections green. When dry, use pipe cleaners for antennae and legs. Have students paint additional features such as eyes, face, etc.

- Many people think a spider is an insect. Use what has been learned about insects to determine if a spider is an insect. If it is not an insect, what is it? Research to find out more about the arthropod grouping of animals. Insects and spiders are both in this group. Determine what animal characteristics insects and spiders have that put each of them in this group.

- Read *The Very Hungry Caterpillar* by Eric Carle to find out about the metamorphosis a caterpillar goes through to become a butterfly. Additional resources related to the life cycle of a butterfly can be found on pages 78 and 79. Help students gain more understanding and knowledge of the actual process of the butterfly life by creating the following project. Give each child a construction paper strip. Direct the children to fold the long strip in half and then in half again to create four sections. Have the children glue a white bean in the center of the first section. At the bottom, let the children write the word *egg*. In the second section, glue a green pipe cleaner which has been bent in a ripple fashion to resemble a caterpillar. Write the word *caterpillar*. To the third section, glue prepared cotton balls. (Preparation: Place the cotton balls in a plastic bag. Pour in a small amount of brown tempera paint powder, seal, and shake. The white cotton balls will turn brown.) Write the word *chrysalis*. Glue a butterfly shape or sticker to the fourth section and write the word *butterfly*. A paper plate divided into four sections can be used as an alternative to the strip of construction paper. In this way, the students can spin the circle to show the life cycle, too.

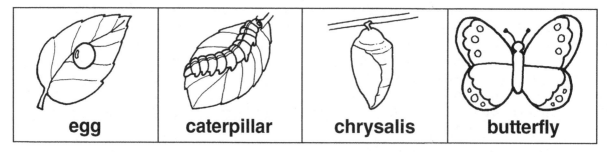

| egg | caterpillar | chrysalis | butterfly |

Suggested Books

Carle, Eric. *The Very Hungry Caterpillar.* Scholastic Paperbacks, 1994.

Heller, Ruth. *Chickens Aren't the Only Ones.* Paper Star, 1999.

Heller, Ruth. *How to Hide a Butterfly and Other Insects.* Price Stern Sloan, 1992.

Kilpatrick, Cathy. *Creepy Crawlies.* E D C Publications, 1994.

Seymour, Peter. *Insects: A Close Up Look.* Simon & Schuster, 1994.

Zemlicka, Shannon. *From Egg to Butterfly.* Lerner Publications Company, 2002.

Parts of a Butterfly

Directions: Cut out the word cards at the bottom of the page. Glue them in the correct places in order to label the diagram.

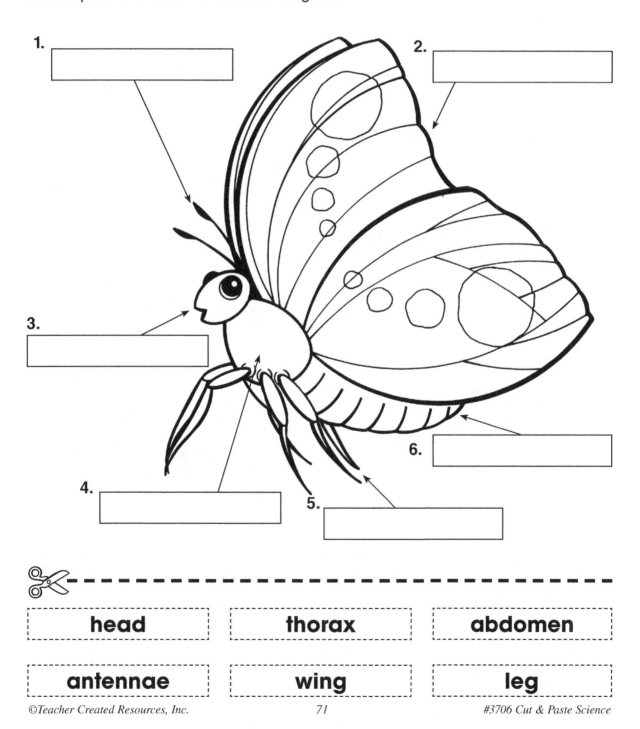

1.

2.

3.

4.

5.

6.

✂ -

| head | thorax | abdomen |

| antennae | wing | leg |

Insect Parts

Directions: Cut out the parts of an insect at the bottom of the page. Glue them in the correct places in order to give each insect picture all the parts of an insect.

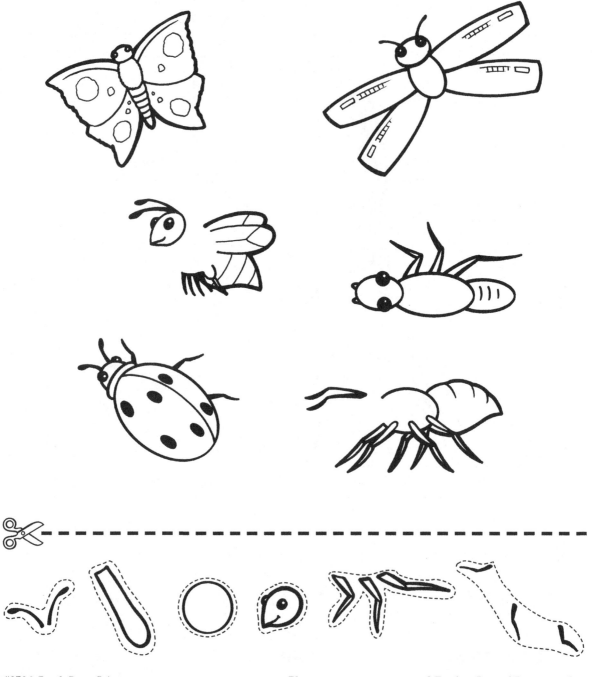

All About Insects

Directions: Cut out the word cards below. Glue them in the correct places in order to complete the sentences.

1. Insects are _____.

2. All insects have six _____.

3. Insects have three _____ parts.

4. Some insects have _____ to help them fly.

5. An insect's feelers are called _____.

6. The body parts of an insect are the _____, the _____, and the _____.

7. A caterpillar is an insect that goes through _____.

✂ ─

| arthropods | metamorphosis |

| legs | wings | antennae | thorax |

| head | body | abdomen |

Life Cycles

Suggested Activities

The best way for students to learn about life cycles is for them to observe a life cycle first hand. Have students keep a journal documenting the changes they see in the animal being observed. Consider the following life cycle choices for your classroom:

- The easiest life cycle to observe is the life cycle of a plant. Provide a plastic cup for each student in your classroom. Fill the cup with dirt. Have each student use his or her pencil or finger to poke a hole in the dirt. Drop a seed inside the hole and cover the hole with dirt. Water appropriately and be sure to provide plenty of sun. Use a seed such as a bean, sunflower, or pumpkin. Students will be excited when they are able to see the flower and then the seeds produced from the plant that will continue the life cycle.

- Create classroom excitement by raising butterflies. Classroom kits can often be purchased through local educational supply stores and catalogs. See addresses below. If your budget does not permit this expense, you may want to build your own. Use scissors to cut off the top portion of an empty, clear plastic soda bottle. Discard this top portion. Fill the bottom of the soda bottle with potting soil (about one-fourth full). Plant a small plant or plant cutting in the soil; moisten the soil. Stand up some twigs close to the leaf. Place the caterpillar on a leaf of the plant. Cover the top of the bottle with aluminum foil and secure with a rubber band. Poke holes in the foil lid for ventilation (a pencil works too). Observe daily. Add water to the plant as needed.

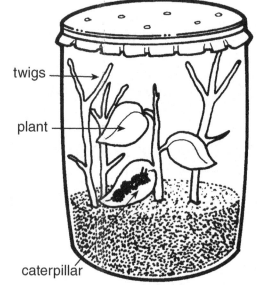

twigs

plant

aluminum foil

caterpillar

soda bottle

- Another interesting life cycle to observe is that of a frog. Obtain a tadpole through an educational supply store or catalog and observe the changes of a tadpole as it matures into a frog. Bringing a tadpole into the classroom is highly recommended because many students have not had the experience of seeing the life cycle of a frog.

Listed below are a number of science supply houses that sell butterfly and tadpole supplies. Please contact the individual companies at the number listed.

Carolina Biological Supply
Call 1-800-334-5551 for a catalog.

Dale Seymour Publications (Pearson Learning Group)
Call 1-800-872-1100 for a catalog.

Delta Education Hands-On Science
Call 1-800-442-5444 for a catalog.

Discovery Channel
Call 1-800-227-1114 for a catalog.

Life Cycles *(cont.)*

Suggested Activities *(cont.)*

- Create a paper chain showing the life cycle of a frog. Cut strips of white paper to 1" x 8 1/2" (2.54 cm x 22 cm). On each strip of paper write down and illustrate one phase in the life cycle of a frog. Begin with laying the eggs and finish with an adult frog. Attach the strips of paper together to form a chain showing the correct sequence of the change from egg to frog. If you wish, connect the final chain back to the first one, forming a circle, showing that the life cycle continues even as the frog is an adult. This activity can be done with the life cycle of any animal. Substitute the animal or plant whose life cycle you are currently working on in place of the frog.

- Divide a paper plate into the number of sections needed for the phases of the life cycle for the animal or plant for which you will be doing this activity. Use a black marker to show the division lines. For example, if you are studying the life cycle of a butterfly, you may want to divide the paper plate into four sections (egg, caterpillar, chrysalis, and butterfly). Show the sequence of the life cycle by either drawing a picture in each section or, if you choose, glue an object into each section to represent that phase of the life cycle. For example, a white bean can represent an egg, a piece of pipe cleaner can represent the caterpillar, a cotton ball can represent the chrysalis, and a sticker of a butterfly can represent the butterfly. Allow your students to be creative; they will think of great objects to represent the phases of the life cycle on which you are working.

- Create a storyboard that shows the sequence of events of a life cycle. Tape a piece of butcher paper to a long table or the wall. Assemble the whole class and ask them to recall the sequence of events of the life cycle on which you are working. Record the events on a separate piece of chart paper in written form and with simple illustrations. Ask the children which event came first, second, etc., until all the events have been accounted for. Make sure that the children are clear on the correct order. Number the events on the paper if necessary. Divide the students into small cooperative groups of three or four and assign each group a phase of the life cycle. Direct the groups to create a map on the butcher paper that illustrates the events of the life cycle. After the first group has illustrated the first event the students continue in the same manner until the life cycle has been completely mapped out. Challenge them to write a sentence or sentences for their events.

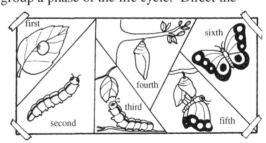

Suggested Books

Carle, Eric. *The Tiny Seed.* Aladdin Paperbacks, 2001.

Gibbons, Gail. *From Seed to Plant.* Holiday House, 1993.

Heiligman, Deborah. *From Caterpillar to Butterfly.* HarperTrophy, 1996.

Pfeffer, Wendy. *From Tadpole to Frog.* HarperTrophy, 1994.

Wallace, Karen. *Tale of a Tadpole.* DK Publishing, 1998.

Zemlicka, Shannon. *From Egg to Butterfly.* Lerner Publishing Group, 2002.

The Life Cycle of a Plant

Directions: Cut out the picture cards at the bottom of the page. Glue them in the correct places to sequence the life cycle of a plant.

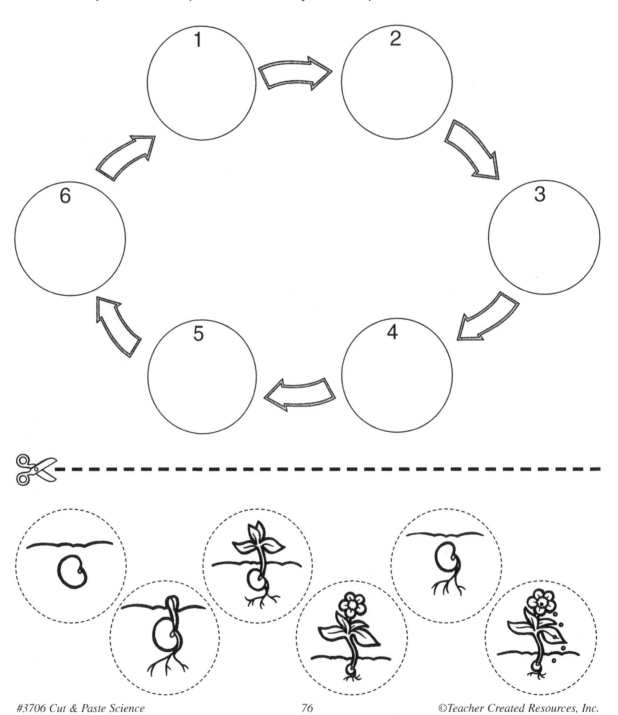

The Life Cycle of a Plant

Directions: Cut out the word cards at the bottom of the page. Glue them in the correct places in order to complete the sentences.

1. Plant a ☐ in the soil and water it.

2. Soon the seed begins to ☐.

3. First, ☐ grow deep into the soil.

4. Next, a ☐ grows up above the ground.

5. A small plant is called a ☐.

6. The ☐ grows up toward the light.

7. ☐ grow from the stem.

8. A flower grows on the plant. The flower has ☐

roots	Leaves	grow	seeds
shoot	stem	sprout	seed

The Life Cycle of a Butterfly

Directions: Cut out the picture cards at the bottom of the page. Glue them in the correct places to sequence the life cycle of a butterfly.

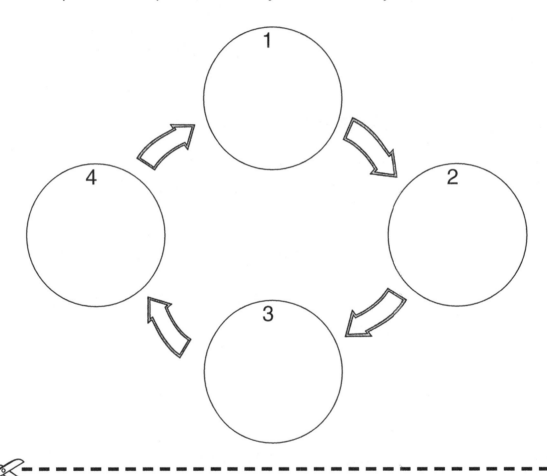

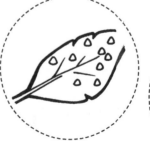

The Life Cycle of a Butterfly

Directions: Cut out the word cards at the bottom of the page. Glue the word cards in the correct places in order to complete the sentences.

1. Some butterflies only lay one _____, while others lay hundreds of them.

2. When the eggs hatch, a _____ emerges.

3. As a caterpillar eats, it _____. It _____ its skin four or five times.

4. When a caterpillar molts for the last time, the caterpillar makes a shell called a _____.

5. A _____ stays in the chrysalis anywhere from two weeks to many months.

6. When a _____ comes out of the chrysalis, it will be damp.

7. It stretches out its wings to dry. After about two hours, it is ready to _____.

8. When the butterfly is old enough, it will fly away to find a _____.

9. Eventually, the _____ will lay her eggs on a leafy plant. The _____ will begin again.

✂ -

egg	caterpillar	female	caterpillar	life cycle
fly	mate	butterfly	molts	chrysalis

grows

The Life Cycle of a Frog

Directions: Cut out the picture cards at the bottom of the page. Glue them in the correct places to sequence the life cycle of a frog.

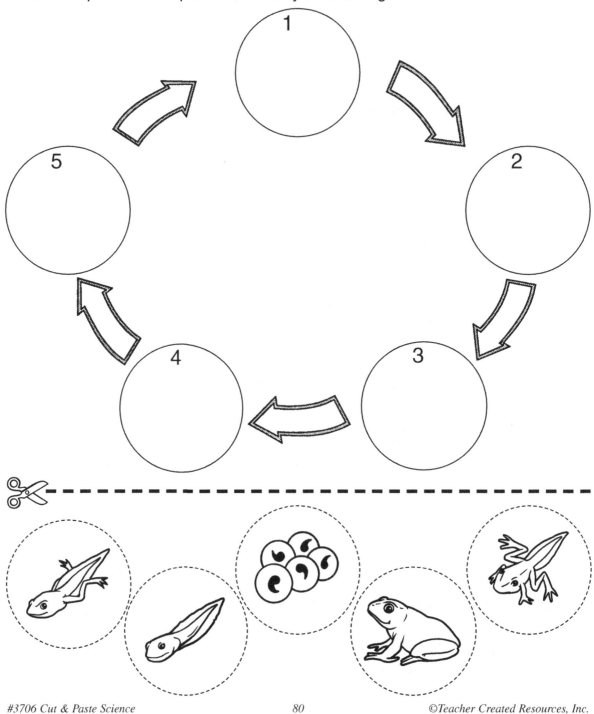

The Life Cycle of a Frog

Directions: Cut out the word cards at the bottom of the page. Glue the word cards in the correct places to complete the sentences.

1. A female frog lays hundreds of _____ at a time. She lays them in the _____.

2. After about ten days, the eggs _____.

3. The _____ live in the water and breathe through _____.

4. The tadpole grows _____.

5. Soon, _____ with fingers grow.

6. As the tadpole grows, its _____ shrinks.

7. A full-grown frog can _____ air and live on _____.

8. When a frog is an adult, it can find a _____. The _____ continues.

✂ —

eggs	**water**	**hatch**	**gills**
mate	**breathe**	**tail**	**life cycle**
arms	**land**	**tadpoles**	**webbed feet**

The Five Senses

Suggested Activities

Below are suggested activities that can be used throughout the unit of study.

- Teach students this tip to help them remember the five senses. Following the directions below, use one hand and add a finger at a time. Hold fingers in place as you use the next finger to add a new sense until all five senses have been named.

Hearing—touch thumb to earlobe

Seeing—touch index finger to eye (warn students not to touch the inside of their eyes)

Smelling—touch middle finger to nose

Tasting—touch ring finger to mouth

Touching—wiggle little finger in the air in front of chin

- Set up a senses learning center or sensory table complete with objects students can explore using their five senses. Allow students to visit the center before, during, and after your study of the senses. Encourage students to use as many of their senses as is safe while exploring each object. Change the objects in the center for variety. Some ideas for objects are listed below.

Sight A variety of usual and unusual objects
Pictures, photographs, artifacts, art reproductions, or posters

Sound A variety of pitches (high and low) and types of sound (music and objects to bang together)
Instruments, sound recordings, music, pots and pans (to bang), keys, toys that make noise

Smell A variety of scents including: pungent, sweet, strong
Cotton balls dipped in cooking extracts, flowers, onions, cabbage, perfume

Taste A variety of tastes including foods that are sweet, sour, bitter, and salty; unusual foods which students may not have tasted
Oranges, pretzels, candy, chips, limes, cranberries, coconut

Touch A variety of textures including: smooth, rough, slippery, bumpy, soft, hard, wet
Burlap, wax paper, feathers, various liquids, rocks, bubble wrap, oil

- Send students on a five senses scavenger hunt. (This can be done at school or as homework.) Have students identify objects that they can experience with all five senses. Provide a variety of objects with which the students can experiment. Students should keep track of which senses they can use to experience each object. Be sure to carefully select the objects placed on the table, as well as have an adult monitoring the activity.

The Five Senses *(cont.)*

Suggested Activities *(cont.)*

- Teach students the poem "The Five Senses." Use the poem to learn more about each of the senses. Have students brainstorm what they do with each sense.

The Five Senses

I use my eyes to help me see,

My nose to help me smell.

I use my tongue to help me taste

The things I love so well.

I use my hands to help me touch,

My ears help me hear sound.

My five senses help me

learn about the world all around.

- Create sensory boxes. Place an object or objects in a shoebox (or brown paper bag) and label it telling students which sense they must use to figure out the contents of the sensory box. For example, label a box "hearing" and then place keys inside the box. Students must shake the box in order to hear the sound the objects make. Students can then make a guess as to the contents of the box before looking to see if they are correct. You may wish to extend the activity by allowing students to use two senses. For example, students can first use their sense of hearing to try to figure out the object and then use their sense of touch to help confirm their guess. Sensory boxes can be created for all five senses. See page 82 for suggestions of objects to place in the boxes.

- Have students use all five senses to experience a coconut. Some students may not know what a coconut is. Chart adjectives and adverbs that can be used to describe the coconut as the class experiences it with all five senses. Begin with the senses of sight, sound, and touch. Then, open the coconut to have students use their senses of smell and taste. You may also choose to have packaged, sweetened coconut available for students to taste.

Suggested Books

Aliki. *My Five Senses.* HarperTrophy, 1990.

Aliki. *My Hands.* Harpercollins Juvenile Books, 1992.

Fowler, Allan. *Smelling Things.* Children's Press, 1991.

Fowler, Allan. *Tasting Things.* Children's Press, 1991.

Showers, Paul. *Your Skin and Mine.* Harpercollins Juvenile Books, 1991.

Naming the Senses

Directions: Cut out the word cards below. Glue them in the correct places so that the five senses are labeled.

1.

2.

3.

4.

5.

6.

✂ --

The Five Senses	eyes (seeing)	ears (hearing)
nose (smelling)	tongue (tasting)	skin (touching)

Which Sense?

Directions: Cut out the picture/word cards at the bottom of the page. Glue the picture/word cards in the places that <u>best</u> labels the senses used to experience each object.

1.

2.

3.

4.

5.

6.

7.

8.

9.

10.

 sight

 taste

 touch

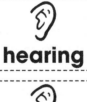 **hearing**

 smell

 sight

 **taste**

 touch

hearing

smell

The Five Senses

Directions: Cut out the word cards at the bottom of the page. Glue the word cards in the correct place in order to complete the sentences.

1. My _____ help me _____ the green grass.

2. I use my _____ to _____ a rose.

3. My _____ is used to _____ food.

4. I _____ my soft teddy bear with my _____.

5. When the car honked its horn, I could _____ it with my _____.

✂ -

eyes	ears	nose	hands	tongue
see	hear	smell	touch	taste

86

The Food Pyramid

Suggested Activities

Below are suggested activities that can be used throughout the unit of study.

- Create an extra large, class food pyramid. Draw a triangle on a large piece of chart paper. Divide the triangle into the sections of the food pyramid. Label each section with the name of the food group and the number of recommended servings. Provide grocery store sales ads and home magazines for the students to look through. Students should cut out food items, determine where to place them on the food pyramid, and then glue them in the correct places. Challenge the students to find a proportional amount of pictures for the recommended servings for each food group. For example, the bread, cereal, rice, and pasta group should have more pictures in it than the fats, oils, and sweets.

- Have students draw a picture and write about their favorite food. Determine from which food group(s) the food comes. Create a class graph showing which food group is most frequently represented by the students' favorite food. How do the results of your class graph compare to the recommended daily servings from the food pyramid? Are the favorite foods in your class represented at the top or bottom of the food pyramid?

- Divide students into groups of 2–4 children. Assign each group an entree that contains food from several food groups (such as hamburgers, pizza, tacos, or spaghetti). Students should work together to determine all of the food groups represented in their assigned dinner. Do the foods that were assigned to each group represent a balanced meal?

- Have students keep a food journal of everything they eat during one day, beginning with breakfast all the way through an evening snack. The next day, have students categorize the foods they ate by the food pyramid groups. Then, ask students to analyze the types and quantities of food they ate in relationship to the recommendations on the food pyramid.

- Divide students into seven groups. Assign each student group a food group on which to work. Have students think of as many food items as possible for their food group. Share the results with the class.

The Food Pyramid *(cont.)*

Suggested Activities *(cont.)*

- Think of some unusual foods such as coconut, escargot, and lamb. Write the names of the foods on index cards, one food item on each index card. Distribute the cards to individuals, pairs, or groups of students. Have students try to categorize these unusual foods into the food pyramid groups. Ask students to be ready to give reasons why they feel their food item belongs in the group they selected.

- For homework, assign students to look through their pantries to find food items with the food pyramid printed on the packaging. If possible, have students bring the food package to class. Create a graph or tally chart to show which food group most often prints the food pyramid on its packaging. Ask the students if the results surprise them. Think of as many reasons as possible to explain your findings.

- Provide a school lunch menu for students to analyze for nutritional content. Have students categorize all of the items that will be served. Determine how many items will be served from each food group. Does the school lunch seem to be a balanced lunch? Does it help students meet the daily food pyramid recommendations for servings? Have students design their own lunch menu. Students should use the food pyramid recommendations to ensure a properly balanced meal.

Suggested Books

Buono, Anthony. *The Race Against Junk Food.* Hcom Inc., 1997.

Haduch, Bill. *Food Rules: The Stuff You Munch, Its Crunch, Its Punch, and Why You Sometimes Lose Your Lunch.* Puffin, 2001.

Kalbacken, Joan. *The Food Pyramid.* Children's Press, 1998.

Leedy, Loreen. *The Edible Pyramid: Good Eating Every Day.* Scott Foresman, 1996.

Rockwell, Lizzy. *Good Enough to Eat: A Kid's Guide to Food and Nutrition.* Harpercollins Juvenile Books, 1999.

The Food Pyramid

Directions: Cut out the picture cards on this page. Glue the picture cards in the correct places on the food pyramid on page 90.

The Food Pyramid *(cont.)*

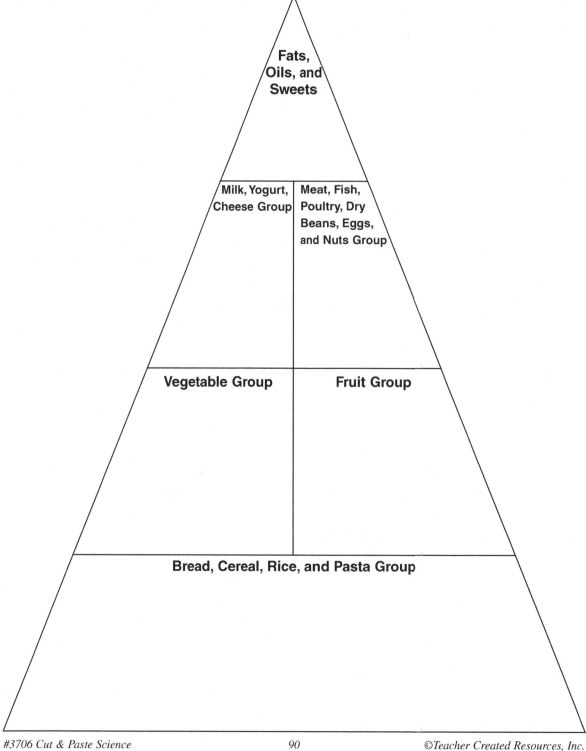

How Much Food?

Directions: Cut out the word cards at the bottom of the page. Glue the word cards in the correct places to complete the table.

	Food Group	Number of Servings
1.	Bread, Cereal, Rice, and Pasta	
2.	Vegetable	
3.		2–4 Servings
4.	Milk, Yogurt, and Cheese	
5.	Meat, Poultry, Fish, Dry Beans, Eggs, and Nuts	
6.		Use Sparingly

3–5 Servings	Fats, Oils, & Sweets	6–11 Servings
2–3 Servings	Fruit Group	2–3 Servings

Eating Advice

Directions: Cut out the word cards at the bottom of the page. Glue the word cards in the correct places in order to complete the sentences.

1. We should eat the most servings from the

   [_____] group.

2. Fats, oils, and sweets should be eaten

   [_____].

3. Carrots, potatoes, broccoli, and peas are in the

   [_____] group.

4. We should have [_____] from both the

   milk, yogurt, and cheese group and the meats,

   poultry, fish, dry beans, eggs, and nuts group.

5. Bananas, apples, and oranges are in the

   [_____] group.

6. The [_____] shows us the kinds and

   amounts of foods we should be eating.

- -

bread, cereals, rice and pasta	sparingly	vegetable
2–3 Servings	**Food Pyramid**	**fruit**

Answer Key

Page 10

1. solid
2. liquid
3. solid
4. liquid
5. liquid
6. gas
7. solid
8. gas

Page 11

Solid: ice cubes, ice that children are skating on
Liquid: glass of water, lake
Gas: steam from teapot, steam from the mouth

Page 12

1. Matter
2. described
3. forms
4. container
5. Solids
6. spread

Page 15

Magnetic: metal whistle, hook, metal spoon, metal screw
Not Magnetic: crayon, shell, plastic ball, wooden block, book, plastic soda bottle

Page 16

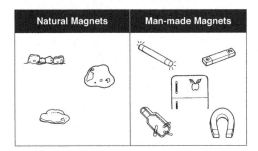

Page 17

1. magnetic
2. demagnetize
3. repel
4. attract
5. magnetic pole
6. magnet

Page 20

1. wedge
2. wheel and axle
3. screw
4. inclined plane
5. lever
6. pulley

Page 21

Wedge: zipper, nail, axe, pocket knife
Lever: hammer, screwdriver, tongs, staple remover, wrench, tweezers

Page 22

1. effort
2. simple machines
3. inclined plane
4. wedge
5. fulcrum
6. lever

Page 25

1. gas
2. heat disk
3. fuse
4. base
5. filament
6. support wires
7. button
8. exhaust tube

Page 26

Connections That Will Light the Bulb	Connections That Will Not Light the Bulb

Page 27

1. static, current
2. alternating, direct
3. Conductors
4. resistors
5. Static
6. lightening
7. complete
8. chemically

Answer Key (cont.)

Page 30
1. rainy
2. sunny
3. windy
4. snowy

Page 31
Sunny Day: Have a picnic, Wear shorts, Go to the park, Climb a tree
Rainy Day: Stomp in puddles, Wear rainboots, Use an umbrella, Float leaves in the water

Page 32
1. sunny, picnic
2. rains, umbrella
3. snowman, snowy
4. kite, windy

Page 35
1. spring
2. summer
3. fall
4. winter

Page 36
Winter: picture of child making a snowman, picture of child with sled
Spring: picture of child with umbrella, picture of child picking flowers
Summer: picture of child swimming, picture of child having a picnic
Fall: picture of child with pumpkin, picture of child raking leaves

Page 37
1. winter
2. summer
3. spring
4. fall
5. hat
6. Shorts
7. sweater
8. jacket

Page 40
1. Crust
2. Mantle
3. Inner Core
4. Outer Core
5. Topsoil

Page 41
1. picture of diamond ring
2. picture of chalk
3. picture of pencil
4. picture of sidewalk
5. picture of table salt
6. picture of brick fence

Page 42
1. Magma
2. erosion
3. Sand
4. Fossils
5. layers
6. classified
7. volcano
8. rocks

Page 45
1. Ash
2. Lava
3. Crust
4. Crater
5. Side Vent
6. Magma Chamber

Page 46

1. A volcano that is peaked is called a **cinder cone volcano**.

2. A **composite volcano's** shape is semi-round.

3. A volcano that is smooth and rounded is called a **shield volcano**.

Page 47
1. volcanoes
2. magma chamber
3. lava
4. crust
5. Side vents
6. crater
7. dormant
8. active

Page 50
Day: picture of child eating cereal, picture of people shopping, picture of people walking, picture of girl skating
Night: picture of a person reading a bedtime story, picture of person going trick-or-treat, picture of person using a flashlight, picture of person sleeping

Answer Key (cont.)

Page 51

1. day   4. night   7. night
2. night   5. night   8. day
3. day   6. day

Page 52

1. day   4. sun   7. moon
2. night   5. heat   8. star
3. night   6. moon

Page 55

1. evaporation   3. rain
2. condensation   4. run-off

Page 56

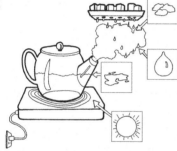

Page 57

1. ocean   5. clouds
2. sun   6. rain
3. evaporates   7. runs off
4. condenses   8. water cycle

Page 60

1. flower   4. seed
2. stem   5. roots
3. leaf

Page 61

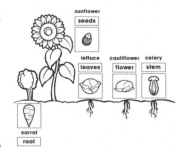

Page 62

1. seed   4. plant   7. Leaves
2. grow   5. leaves   8. flower
3. roots   6. stem

Page 66

Mammals: raccoon, elephant, dog
Birds: robin, hummingbird, eagle
Arthropods: dragonfly, butterfly, ladybug
Reptiles: snake, turtle, lizard
Fish: shark, salmon, trout
Amphibians: salamander, toad, frog
Mollusks: snail, slug, octopus

Page 67

Warm Blooded: mammals, birds
Cold Blooded: reptiles, fish, amphibians
Backbone: mammals, birds, fish, amphibians, reptiles
Lay Eggs: birds, reptiles, arthropods, fish, amphibians
Have Wings: birds
No Backbone: arthropods, mollusks

Page 68

1. milk   5. water, land
2. feathers, fly 6. spine
3. skin   7. segmented, exoskeleton
4. Fish

Page 71

1. antennae   4. thorax
2. wing   5. leg
3. head   6. abdomen

Page 72

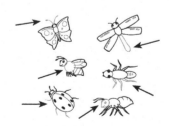

Page 73

1. arthropods   5. antennae
2. legs   6. head, thorax, abdomen
3. body   7. metamorphosis
4. wings

Answer Key *(cont.)*

Page 76

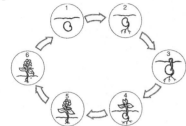
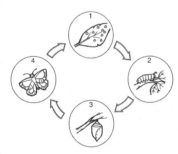

Page 77

1. seed
2. grow
3. roots
4. shoot
5. sprout
6. stem
7. Leaves
8. seeds

Page 78

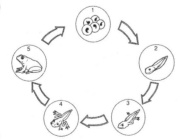

Page 79

1. egg
2. caterpillar
3. grows, molts
4. chrysalis
5. caterpillar
6. butterfly
7. fly
8. mate
9. female, life cycle

Page 80

Page 81

1. eggs, water
2. hatch
3. tadpoles, gills
4. webbed feet
5. arms
6. tail
7 breathe, land
8. mate, life cycle

Page 84

1. The Five Senses
2. eyes (seeing)
3. ears (hearing)
4. nose (smelling)
5. tongue (tasting)
6. skin (touching)

Page 85

Suggested answers:

1. smell
2. touch
3. sight
4. taste
5. hearing
6. taste
7. hearing
8. sight
9 smell
10. touch

Page 86

1. eyes, see
2. nose, smell
3. tongue, taste
4. touch, hands
5. hear, ears

Page 90

Fats, Oils, and Sweets: taffy, chips, chocolate bar

Milk, Yogurt, Cheese Group: cheese, yogurt, milk

Meat, Fish, Poultry, Dry Beans, Eggs, and Nuts Group: eggs, steak

Vegetable Group: carrot, broccoli, celery

Fruit Group: apple, banana, grapes, strawberry

Bread, Cereal, Rice, and Pasta Group: bread, cereal, spaghetti

Page 91

1. 6–11 Servings
2. 3–5 Servings
3. Fruit Group
4. 2–3 Servings
5. 2–3 Servings
6. Fats, Oils, & Sweets

Page 92

1. bread, cereals, rice, and pasta
2. sparingly
3. vegetable
4. 2–3 servings
5. fruit
6. Food Pyramid

Made in the USA
Coppell, TX
05 March 2022

74493587R00057